LEARNING'S OF MINE: I

VOLUME I: THE FIRST STEP

GUNJAN BHONDE

Made with ♥ on the Notion Press Platform
www.notionpress.com

LEARNING'S OF MINE: I

Volume I: The First Step

The Original Work By

Gunjan Bhonde

The losers of the mind, the winners of the mind, win.

Contents

The ice was once water,
The devil was once an angel,
Anger was once love,
The loudest voice was once silent,
An introvert was once an extrovert.

"There is nothing in this world that can take the place of stubbornness"

ix

Preface

Hi there! If you're reading this book, consider yourself a lucky person. Allow me to introduce myself, my name is Gunjan Bhonde. By Education, I am an electrical engineer, but I have a deep passion for Sci-fi movies and documentaries. In my free time, I enjoy the art of miniature crafting.

Now, you might be wondering, why am I writing this book?

The answer is simple: I am naturally curious and have a relentless desire to discover new things and keep learning. I believe that knowledge is meant to be shared, and I probably know something that you might find interesting. This book is my way of sharing what I've learned with you.

You may also be asking, what makes this book different from others?

Well, I hope that after reading it, you'll find the answer. I've put in a lot of thought and effort to offer you a unique perspective, something that stands out from the crowd.

And finally, you might wonder, will this book add to your knowledge?

In my opinion, I've done my best to deliver as much value as I can. It's my sincere hope that you find this book both insightful and enriching.

So, let's dive in and begin this exciting journey!

Acknowledgements

This book, *Learning's of Mine: I*, is not just a culmination of my thoughts and experiences but also the first in a series of books that delve into the lesson's life has taught me, shaped by encouragement, support, and inspiration I have received from many people along the way.

First and foremost, I want to thank my family for being my constant pillars of strength and love. Your unwavering support has always fueled my aspirations and kept me grounded, and for that, I am deeply grateful.

To my friends and mentors who believed in me even when I doubted myself thank you for your guidance, constructive criticism, and encouragement. Your words of wisdom have helped shape my journey, and your belief in me has made this book possible.

To the countless people, stories, and moments in life that have taught me lessons, directly or indirectly thank you. Every interaction, every challenge, and every triumph has contributed to the thoughts and reflections within these pages.

A special thanks to all the readers who have chosen to pick up this book. Your time and trust mean the world to me. It is my sincere hope that the words in this book resonate with you and offer value in your own journey of learning and growth.

Finally, I am deeply grateful to the universal force that guides us all the force that inspires creativity, grants clarity, and connects us to one another.

This book is a testament to the power of collective experiences, and I dedicate it to everyone who has contributed to mine.

With heartfelt gratitude,

Gunjan B. Bhonde

CHAPTER I

The Probability of Life on Earth

However, in reality, it is an immensely vast and deeply complex topic, encompassing not only what happened after the Big Bang but also the events that may have preceded it. The probability of life, particularly the formation of proteins and other essential components, adds another layer of intricacy. It is nearly impossible to cover everything in detail within a single book. For the sake of understanding, I've simplified this topic into a short note.

As we move on to the first topic, let me ask you, do you know what probability is? If not, let me explain. Consider this as a challenge: take a coin, flip it in the air, and choose one side of the coin, let's say *heads*, for ten flips. Imagine you're predicting that you'll get *heads* all ten times. Now, go ahead and flip the coin ten times. Did you get heads all ten times, as you imagined? Most likely, no. But why not? Why is it so unlikely to get heads ten times in a row? This happens because the probability of each flip being heads is 1/2 (or 50%), and the chances of getting *heads* consistently for ten flips decrease exponentially. The more flips you add, the harder it becomes to achieve the same outcome repeatedly. Understanding this concept of probability will help you figure out why such outcomes are improbable in practice!

Have you ever wondered about the probability of life? If your answer is no, then congratulations! You're in the right place. We will begin by discussing this fascinating question.

So, let's get started!

The probability of life on Earth is nothing short of extraordinary a cosmic miracle woven from an intricate alignment of factors that make our planet a unique oasis in the vast, mysterious expanse of space. Have you ever stopped to marvel at how everything seems to fit together so perfectly? Earth sits in the "Goldilocks Zone," that sweet spot just the right distance from the Sun, where temperatures are neither too hot nor too cold, allowing liquid water to exist a cornerstone for life as we know it. Imagine if we were just a little closer or farther away life might never have had a chance to take root.

But it doesn't stop there. Earth's stable orbit is like a perfectly timed dance, preventing extreme temperature swings that would otherwise make life unbearable. Our atmosphere, a magical blend of oxygen and nitrogen, not only sustains life but also acts as a shield, protecting us from the Sun's harmful radiation. It's like Earth itself wrapped us in an invisible blanket, keeping us safe.

And then there's Earth's magnetic field, born from the restless churning of its molten iron core. Think of it as an invisible force field, deflecting deadly solar winds that would strip away our atmosphere if left unchecked. Without it, the very air we breathe would be gone. Beneath our feet, the geological activity volcanic eruptions and plate tectonics may seem chaotic and destructive, but they play a vital role in recycling nutrients, maintaining fertile soils, and stabilizing the climate over millennia. These "violent" acts of nature are, in truth, the heartbeat of our planet, ensuring life continues to thrive.

Even the Moon has a part to play in this grand story. Its gravitational pull stabilizes Earth's axial tilt, giving us consistent seasons. Without it, our world might wobble unpredictably, plunging into environmental chaos. Imagine a world without stable seasons how would life have evolved?

And what about water? The Sun powers Earth's water cycle, connecting oceans, rivers, rain, and clouds in a delicate, life-giving rhythm. Every drop of water you've ever seen is part of a system that has existed for billions of years, sustaining everything from the smallest microbes to the most complex ecosystems.

Yet, when we step back and consider the size and age of the universe, the probability of all these factors aligning perfectly on one tiny planet feels astronomically small. Think about it: billions of galaxies, trillions of planets, and somehow, Earth hit the cosmic jackpot. It's like winning the universe's rarest lottery ticket.

But here's the twist in the story the vastness of the cosmos also leaves room for hope. With so many stars and planets out there, could Earth truly be the only world where life exists? Astronomers have discovered exoplanets orbiting distant stars, some with conditions that might support life. Perhaps somewhere out there, on a planet bathed in a light we'll never see, other beings wonder about their place in the universe, just as we do.

For now, though, Earth remains the only known haven for life. It's a reminder of how precious and fragile our existence is. It's easy to take it all for granted the sunrise, the rain, the air we breathe but every moment of life is a gift from this miraculous planet.

And so, the story of Earth isn't just about science; it's about us. It's about our responsibility to protect and preserve this one-of-a-kind home. Because in the grand cosmic lottery, we are the winners. And it's up to us to ensure that this incredible story of life continues for generations to come.

Chandra Wickramasinghe the British mathematician and astronomer, along with his collaborator Fred Hoyle, has advanced the panspermia hypothesis, that proposes that life on Earth is, at least in part, of extraterrestrial origin.

I often find myself wondering why everything around us seems to fit so perfectly, almost as if life and nature are part of a grand design. Is it possible that we are not native to Earth, that perhaps we once lived on another planet before calling this one home? Or is everything we see the intricate balance of nature, the harmony in its processes a product of natural creation? Could it be the work of a predefined creator, someone or something that designed human beings and all that exists?

This book is written by me, which makes me its author. Once it is published, the publishing house becomes its creator in a broader sense. This brings me to a profound question: if everything has a creator, who created us? If, for a moment, we accept the idea that God created us, another question immediately arises who created God? After all, if everything has a creator, shouldn't the same rule apply to God?

There are two prevailing perspectives on this matter. The first is randomness, and the second is design. If you believe in randomness, you are likely an atheist, viewing existence as a series of probabilistic events without a predefined purpose. On the other hand, if you believe in design, you likely believe in God or a higher power responsible for the intricacies of life and the universe.

In my opinion, there is no true randomness; everything operates under the laws of nature. However, this raises yet another question: are the laws of nature themselves a product of randomness, or were they intentionally set by a creator? If a creator exists, who then created the creator? This question remains unresolved and endlessly debated.

Many scientists argue that both God and the laws of nature are eternal, existing beyond the boundaries of creation and destruction. If there is a creator, it is possible that they conceived the universe in a single moment of thought, and it came into existence almost like the snap of Thanos' fingers. Perhaps God imagined the universe, and in that moment, it became reality. While we may never fully understand the origins of existence, this possibility invites us to explore the mysteries of creation and our place within it.

Osho once said that if you ask a theist about God, they will confidently declare, *"There is a God, and I have faith in Him."* On the other hand, if you ask an atheist, they will assert, *"I do not believe in God; this is my faith."* But Buddha offers a unique perspective he says that both the theist and the atheist are, in their own ways, devotees of God. The theist agrees with the existence of God, while the atheist denies it. Yet, Buddha suggests that neither of them is truly religious in the deepest sense.

True religiosity, according to Buddha, lies not in blind faith or denial but in a spirit of honest inquiry. The one who says, *"I do not know whether God exists or not. I am in the dark, and I must seek the truth for myself,"* embodies the essence of a seeker. This individual does not rely on assumptions or unverified beliefs but instead embraces the mystery of existence and commits to a journey of discovery.

How can one claim the existence or non-existence of God without first undertaking this exploration? To assert either claim prematurely is to foreclose the possibility of genuine understanding. The seeker recognizes that the truth will only emerge through their own search, through direct experience. Whatever it may be, comes later after the light of discovery illuminates the darkness. Until then, the seeker remains open, unburdened by the need to affirm or deny, driven only by the quest for truth.

Where do you go to find God? There is no residence, no fixed address where you can seek Him. In truth, no one can directly meet God through mere effort or desire. Instead, when the time is right, God comes to meet the individual there is no other way.

This meeting is not about material pursuits or fulfilling wishes. It is a sacred encounter that transcends worldly desires. Only when you are ready when your heart is free of selfish intentions, when you stand with purity and humility can you experience the divine presence. To find God, you must let go of expectations and accept yourself fully as you are. In this state of genuine acceptance and surrender, you will discover the essence of God within and all around you.

The truth is, I don't have the answers right now. I find myself caught in the age-old debate of whether God exists or not, and honestly, I'm still searching for clarity. But here's what I believe: the journey to understanding these profound questions is deeply personal. Each of us must seek out our own answers, explore our own beliefs, and come to terms with the mysteries of existence in our own way.

People believe in God, and often, this belief is blind. If you truly know something, you do not need to believe in it you simply know it. For instance, you don't believe in the existence of the Earth, soil, or air because their presence is evident and undeniable. They are tangible and experienced in everyday life. However, belief in God is different; it relies on faith rather than evidence. Similarly, concepts like heaven and hell are constructs rooted in belief, often described as realms beyond life. But who has truly seen them? To know what lies in heaven or hell, one would first need to die to experience it. Until then, these ideas remain speculative, almost fictional, shaped by human imagination and tradition. This raises an important question: are these beliefs grounded in truth, or are they simply the stories we tell ourselves to make sense of the unknown?

Many times, I find myself grappling with a profound question: if God created us if there is one supreme entity then why do we have so many religions in the world, each with its own gods and rituals? Is God divided by continents, cultures, or merely by our beliefs? Why have humans developed different concepts of God based on their desires, needs, and perspectives? Perhaps God differentiated humans not by religion, but by their unique identities, behaviors, and circumstances. However, humans themselves have become their own enemies, creating divisions that God never intended.

Think about it if God truly wanted to differentiate humans, wouldn't He have given us vastly distinct features, such as different colors of blood or uniquely functioning organs? Instead, all humans share the same fundamental structure: the same bodies, the same organs, and the same processes. If God intended to divide us by religion, wouldn't He have marked us with a symbol of our faith at birth, a sign that clearly indicated which religion we belonged to? But He didn't.

This suggests that religion and the divisions it creates are human constructs, not divine intentions. God's work is evident in the natural diversity of our appearances, our thoughts, and our experiences. The differences we see in our faces, skin tones, and circumstances are reflections of individuality, not division. Yet, instead of embracing this diversity, humans have used it to create barriers. The idea of religion, instead of uniting us in reverence for a higher power, has often been wielded as a tool for separation. Perhaps the true essence of God lies not in rituals or symbols, but in our shared humanity, compassion, and the ability to coexist harmoniously despite our differences.

Aniruddhacharya Ji Maharaj profoundly said, *"Whoever is born as a human in this world cannot live without dharma."* Dharma, often translated as righteousness or moral duty, is what gives human life its higher purpose and meaning. He explains that dharma is the very principle that distinguishes humans from animals.

For instance, the way you perceive and treat your wife, your mother, and your sister is not the same. Who taught you to differentiate between these relationships? It is dharma that establishes these distinctions and guides you to respect them accordingly. Dharma is the moral compass that defines boundaries, sets norms, and fosters harmony within society.

If we eliminate dharma, the essential difference between human and animal life disappears. Without dharma, life would lack structure, ethics, and a sense of higher responsibility. Animals live by instinct, but humans are endowed with the ability to discern, to differentiate right from wrong, and to uphold values. Dharma is not merely a religious concept; it is the foundation of humanity itself, shaping our thoughts, actions, and relationships. It elevates us beyond mere survival and allows us to live with purpose and dignity.

I often see people tirelessly searching for God in various places, traveling far and wide as though God requires a specific location to establish His presence. Let me clarify I'm not suggesting that you shouldn't visit these sacred places or embark on spiritual journeys. What I'm questioning is the belief that God resides only in these places, as if He's calling out, "Come here, I belong to this place. Visit me, and take my blessings with you." Is that the true essence of God?

Those who undergo a transformation in consciousness find God everywhere not confined to temples or statues but present in every atom of creation. Such individuals do not need a specific place of worship to feel connected to the divine; their awareness turns the entire world into a sacred space.

On the other hand, simply visiting a temple does not make one truly religious. It is not the act of entering a temple that signifies devotion but the realization of one's inner divinity. Those who discover themselves in the quiet sanctity of a temple and recognize the divine within are the ones truly walking a spiritual path.

Worshiping a statue without understanding the essence of God limits the vastness of the divine. True religion lies in perceiving God in every form and every place, not in believing that the divine is confined to a single idol or structure. If one assumes that God exists only within a statue, they miss the broader truth. The divine does not dwell solely in one form; it permeates all of existence. To confine God to a single entity or place is to misunderstand the infinite nature of the divine. True devotion lies in seeing the sacred in everything, everywhere.

If you're living a life filled with harm hurting others, mistreating animals, or creating misery for your own selfish desires and yet expect blessings from God, then my friend, you are deeply mistaken. Remember, what you think is what you become. If you truly wish to find God, begin by looking within yourself. Ask yourself: *Am I living in alignment with values that are good for me and others? Or am I merely putting on a show to gain society's approval? Am I being honest in my actions? Am I harming others emotionally or manipulating them for my own benefit?*

If the answers to these questions reveal wrongdoing, then no amount of visiting holy places, performing acts of charity, or public displays of piety will bring you closer to God. True divinity doesn't reside in rituals or appearances; it resides in our actions, intentions, and the goodness we bring to the world.

God helps those who help themselves and others. If you live with kindness, integrity, and compassion, then you'll find God not in a faraway temple or shrine, but within your own heart. Conversely, if your actions are harmful and insincere, even visiting the holiest of places a hundred times will not bring you closer to divine grace. God's blessings are earned through a life well-lived, not through a façade of spirituality.

I see God in every place, from within myself to the smallest atom in the world. God is not confined to temples, churches, or specific locations; He exists everywhere, permeating all that we see and feel. Whether in the beauty of nature, the innocence of a child, or the vastness of the universe, God's presence is undeniable.

You don't need to embark on a long journey or search far and wide to find God. The divine resides within you, in every breath you take, and in the intricate design of life itself. God exists in the tiniest details, in the stillness of a moment, and in the vast interconnectedness of everything around us.

All you need is the willingness to discover this truth to open your heart, observe the world with clarity, and feel the divinity within yourself and in every corner of existence. God is not a distant being to be found; He is the essence of everything that already is.

Have you ever wondered what you would ask for if you had the chance to meet God? Imagine standing before the divine, overwhelmed with awe and amazement, knowing that God could grant you anything you desire be it a grand mansion, endless wealth, infinite life, or anything beyond imagination. At that moment, take a pause and truly place yourself in that situation. What would you ask for? If you still find yourself searching for a wish to request, perhaps it reveals something deeper that you do not fully believe in God, but rather see God as merely a medium to fulfill your desires. When you treat God as a wish-granter, you risk reducing the divine presence to nothing more than a transaction. True faith lies not in asking for material things but in understanding and embracing God's guidance, purpose, and grace. If you truly believe in God, you would seek not just gifts but the wisdom to live a meaningful and fulfilling life. God's presence itself is the greatest gift, for in that divine connection, you realize that everything you truly need is already within you.

If you choose to ask God for a wish, whether it be for unlimited money, eternal life, or something else, it raises a profound question: are you prioritizing material desires over the presence of God? Does this mean you value wealth, longevity, or possessions more than the divine essence itself? If so, are you truly a follower of God, or are you merely waiting for an opportunity to fulfill your own desires under the guise of devotion?

Ask yourself honestly are you seeking a deeper connection with God, or is your faith conditional, tied to what you can gain from it? True devotion lies not in making requests, but in surrendering oneself to the divine presence and finding contentment in its purity. If your focus remains on worldly gains, then perhaps it is time to reflect on the authenticity of your faith and the intentions behind your prayers.

In my opinion, God bestows upon us three fundamental gifts: **force**, **mind**, and **knowledge**. These are the core elements of human existence, the divine essence that empowers us to navigate life. Force gives us the strength to act, to endure challenges, and to overcome obstacles. The mind is the tool through which we think, reason, and make choices. Knowledge, the illumination of understanding, enables us to discern, grow, and create meaning in our lives.

Everything else we achieve or experience in life stems from these three gifts. Success, happiness, love, and material accomplishments are not separate entities but are outcomes of how we harness this divine force, apply our minds, and expand our knowledge. These gifts are both a responsibility and a blessing, guiding us to live purposefully and contribute meaningfully to the world around us.

Many people engage in charity to showcase their ability to contribute to the lives of others. However, human nature often seeks some form of exchange, even if unspoken. For instance, when wealthy individuals give money to the poor, they might believe they are earning blessings in return. This raises an important question: who, in reality, is the truly poor person? The poor seek money for basic necessities like food and shelter, but if the wealthy give money with the expectation of receiving blessings or recognition, then, in a sense, the rich become the truly poor impoverished in their intent and understanding of selfless giving.

Charity, at its core, should be free from expectations. True charity does not involve seeking gratitude, recognition, or blessings in return. It stems from a genuine desire to help without any thought of personal gain. I do not oppose charity, but I firmly believe that for it to be meaningful, it must come from a place of pure intention. Real charity is giving without expecting anything in return, not even a blessing. Only then can it truly uplift both the giver and the receiver.

In times, humans have created successful and well-known business models by leveraging the names of gods. If a divine being exists in the universe and observes these activities, one might wonder what they would think. It is conceivable that the divine presence, seeing such commercialization of sacred names, could feel a sense of disappointment or concern. The use of these revered names for profit may be seen as a distortion of their original purpose, which was not intended for material gain but for spiritual guidance, solace, and enlightenment. Such actions might invoke a reflection on humanity's priorities whether they have strayed from the path of genuine faith and respect, substituting reverence with exploitation. In this context, one might question the balance between tradition and commercialization, and whether this trend is fostering a deeper connection with the divine or merely capitalizing on belief for personal gain.

The probability of life existing on any given planet, including Earth, is an astonishingly rare. Think about that for a moment out of the countless worlds scattered across the universe, the conditions that make life possible are almost non-existent. Yet, against all odds, here we are. Earth, our incredible home, beat the cosmic lottery to become the cradle of life.

So, take a moment to congratulate yourself your part of the miraculous. You're living proof that even in the face of impossible odds, life finds a way.

• • •

The next time you feel discouraged, overwhelmed, or unmotivated, remember this: you're not just lucky you're extraordinary. You exist on a planet so rare, so unique, that it defies the vast probabilities of the universe. Life itself is a gift, and you're a part of it.

You are the result of billions of years of cosmic, biological, and geological miracles. Never forget you're one in a trillion, living on the one-in-a-million planet called Earth. So, hold your head high and embrace the wonder of your existence, because you are truly special.

• • •

CHAPTER II

Life Begins in Darkness

A place where no light exists, where silence reigns, and the world seems still it is in these hidden depths, within the shadows, that the spark of existence is first kindled. For every living being, life begins in the dark, wrapped in mystery, nurtured by forces unseen.

For us as humans, this journey starts in the darkness of the womb a sanctuary both secure and unknown. Encased in the warm, protective cocoon of our mother's body, we begin as something impossibly small, fragile, and unformed. Each heartbeat, each cell dividing, each fluttering movement slowly builds the foundation of the person we will one day become. In this sacred darkness, we are not alone. We are cradled by a life force that connects us to the vast tapestry of existence. It is in this silence, within the unseen, that life takes its first breathless steps.

And yet, life's beginning in darkness is not a story exclusive to humans. In nature, too, the most beautiful creations begin in the shadows. A tiny seed, buried in the soil, lies dormant and unseen. To the outside world, it appears lifeless, insignificant. But hidden beneath the surface, it is alive with possibility, quietly gathering strength. The soil, dark and rich, cradles the seed, nurturing it with unseen nutrients. The seed splits open, its first roots pushing downward in search of stability while its tender shoot reaches upward toward the light. Without this initial darkness this unseen world there would be no towering trees, no blooming flowers, no lush forests.

Even the stars, those breathtaking jewels scattered across the night sky, owe their existence to the darkness. Before they shine their light, stars are born in dense, dark clouds of gas and dust, hidden from view. It is from this cosmic darkness that they ignite, burning brightly against the void of space. The universe itself began in darkness a silent, infinite expanse before the first spark of the

Big Bang brought light into being. Without the emptiness, the void, there could be no creation.

But life's relationship with darkness is not only physical; it is deeply metaphorical. As human beings, we often face our own moments of darkness times of uncertainty, fear, or despair. These periods can feel endless, as though we are trapped beneath an unyielding weight. Yet, just as seeds grow in the soil and stars emerge from the void, we too grow in our moments of darkness. It is in these times of struggle that we discover our inner strength, our resilience, and our capacity to transform. Darkness, far from being an end, is often the beginning of something greater.

Consider the times when you've felt lost or overwhelmed. Perhaps it was the loss of a loved one, the end of a relationship, or a period of doubt about your purpose in life. In those moments, it might have felt as though the world had stopped, as if you were stuck in an unlit room with no way out. But then, slowly, something began to shift. Maybe it was a conversation with a friend, a sudden burst of inspiration, or simply the quiet passage of time. Like a seed breaking through the soil, you found your way toward the light. Those dark times didn't destroy you they shaped you. They taught you who you are and what you're capable of.

• • •

"Sometimes when you're in a dark place you think you've been buried but you've actually been planted"
| Christine Caine, Australian activist and evangelist

• • •

Life, in its very essence, begins as a spark of creation. In humans, it starts with a single fertilized cell a zygote. This tiny, microscopic entity contains the entire blueprint for what will become a fully formed individual. It divides, multiplies, and organizes itself into a symphony of growth. Organs take shape, tissues develop, and systems come to life, all within the protective darkness of the womb. This same process unfolds across the natural world. A seed germinates, an egg hatches, and a caterpillar emerges from its cocoon, each beginning its unique journey.

Every beginning is a moment of boundless potential. A newborn baby takes its first breath, its tiny lungs filling with air for the first time. A chick breaks free from its shell, stepping into a world it has never seen. A plant unfurls its first leaves, reaching toward the sun. In these moments, life is filled with curiosity, vulnerability, and the unstoppable drive to grow.

But the beginning of life is more than just an individual event. It is a thread in the larger tapestry of existence, connecting the past to the future. Each new life, whether human, animal, or plant, is part of an ongoing cycle of renewal. The seed that becomes a tree may one day fall, its leaves decomposing into the soil to nourish new growth. The child who takes their first steps will one day teach their own children to walk. Life is a continuous flow, a river that never truly stops, carrying with it the promise of renewal.

In this interconnected cycle, every new beginning is both an echo of the past and a promise for the future. Each birth, each sprouting seed, each first breath is a reminder of life's incredible resilience. It shows us that even in the face of darkness, there is always the potential for light.

So, as you think about the beginning of life whether it's the life of a human being, a plant, or a star remember this: every start is a miracle. Every moment of creation carries within its infinite possibilities. And every journey, no matter how uncertain or challenging, begins with a spark. It is in the quiet darkness, the unseen and the unknown, that the greatest stories of life are written. From that spark, an entire universe of growth, discovery, and transformation unfolds.

• • •

In the end, life's beginnings are not just biological or physical events. They are deeply symbolic a testament to the fact that from nothing, something extraordinary can emerge. Darkness is not to be feared; it is to be embraced, for it is there, in the silence, that life truly begins.

· · ·

16

CHAPTER III

The Birth

As you're reading this book, let's pause for a moment. Look at yourself not just physically, but as a conscious being. Your mind is processing these words, your body is alive and functioning, and somewhere deep inside, a question might already be forming: Why me? Why was I born in human form? Why not as a bird soaring high above the clouds, a fish swimming in the ocean's depths, or a tree standing tall and ancient? As you're reading these words, you know English or probably know more than three to four languages but have you ever wondered why you know English? Why not any other language, and what led you to this moment? Why did you emerge as a human, blessed or burdened with consciousness, self-awareness, and the capacity to ask such questions?

To begin, think about your birth. You didn't ask to be born. You didn't choose your parents, your gender, your skin color, or the language you speak. You didn't get to decide whether you'd be born into wealth or poverty, in a bustling city or a remote village. The moment you entered this world; your circumstances were already written by forces far beyond your control. And yet, here you are a living, breathing human being.

Isn't that extraordinary? The sheer randomness of your existence is staggering. The odds of your specific parents meeting, their genetic material combining in just the right way to create *you*, are almost incomprehensible. Go back further, to your ancestors every one of them had to survive long enough to pass on their genes. Think of the moments, the coincidences, the near-misses in history that led to your family line continuing, culminating in you, here, now, reading these words.

What if one thing had been different? What if your great-grandparents had never met? What if a war or a disease had interrupted the delicate thread of life that stretches back through time to the very first humans? You might not exist at all. And even if you did, you might be someone entirely different. A child born in a different country, under a different sky, speaking another language, living another life.

We are all, in a way, accidental products of life a result of countless random combinations of circumstances and biology. At the time of our creation, no one truly knows what we will become whether we will be a boy or a girl, or any of the infinite possibilities that life holds. These combinations are beyond our control, yet they define our existence.

Our lives, however, are not just random outcomes. They carry immense potential and meaning, shaped by the experiences we encounter and the choices we make. Each life is unique, woven from a tapestry of uncertainties, yet it holds the power to influence and inspire. Life, in all its unpredictability, is a gift meant to be embraced and lived with purpose.

Life is much like a bridge, with two ends: a beginning and an ending. Just as a traveler crosses a bridge without fully knowing what lies at either end, we, too, traverse life without knowledge of its ultimate boundaries. Where you are born is beyond your control, and the time, place, and circumstances of your death remain a mystery. If these fundamental truths are unknowable, then why let worry consume you?

From me to you, a heartfelt request: never argue with your parents or create trouble for them in their efforts. Remember, they are your parents the generation before you and it is through them that you exist. Never utter words like, ***"Why did you give me life?"*** because they have always done their best with the knowledge and resources, they had at the time to provide for you and shape your future.

If you ever find yourself upset with your parents or feel like they have fallen short, I urge you to visit an orphanage. There, you will truly understand the immense value of having parents who love and care for you. While no parent is perfect, they work tirelessly to ensure a better life for you a life better than the one they had to endure. Their sacrifices stem from a deep desire to see you succeed and thrive in this world.

All your parents truly seek is your love and support. If you ever face challenges or have doubts, don't criticize them or push them away. Instead, talk to them, share your concerns, and work together to find solutions. Open communication fosters understanding, and your respect and gratitude will mean more to them than you can imagine.

Remember, my friend, your parents care for you more than anyone else in this entire universe. Their love and concern for you are unmatched, rooted in a bond that is selfless and enduring. They have dedicated their lives to your well-being, often putting your needs above their own. In moments of doubt or hardship, always remember the depth of their care and the sacrifices they make for you. Their love is a constant, unwavering force, and no one else can ever replicate the genuine concern and affection they have for you.

But what if you hadn't been born human at all? Imagine for a moment that you were born as a bird, gliding effortlessly through the air, feeling the wind rush past your feathers. Would you long for the consciousness and complexity of being human? Or would you simply live as a bird does, free from the burden of self-awareness? Or what if you were a tree? Rooted to the earth, feeling the sun's warmth on your leaves, your branches reaching toward the sky. Would you miss the ability to reflect on your existence, or would the stillness and simplicity of being a tree feel like enough?

You see, your humanity is as much a product of chance as anything else. Your ability to think, to feel, to question your existence these are uniquely human traits. But what if they're merely the result of a cosmic accident? What if, in another universe, there's a version of *you* that exists as a star burning in the night sky, or as a fish swimming in an ocean so vast it never knows its boundaries?

What is the Purpose of Life?

What if there is no grand purpose to life? What if life itself is the purpose? Life, in its purest form, does not need an external purpose to validate its existence. This question often arises because we fail to recognize and appreciate the sheer grandeur of life. It comes up because we have not yet realized the immensity and beauty of what it truly means to be human.

Life is not something ordinary it is magnificent, extraordinary, and beyond comprehension. The very fact that we exist, that we can think, feel, and experience, is itself a miracle. To search for a purpose beyond life is to overlook the profound gift of being alive. It is to miss the marvel of existence that unfolds in every breath, every heartbeat, and every moment.

Life is not about achieving something outside of itself. It is about experiencing the fullness of being human the joy, the pain, the love, the growth, and the infinite possibilities that come with it. It is too fabulous, too fantastic to be limited by a single purpose. Perhaps, instead of seeking a reason for life, we should simply immerse ourselves in its wonders and allow its magnificence to speak for itself.

Nobody ever asks if you want to be born, and it is not a decision that rests in your hands. One day, without any choice of your own, you find yourself in the midst of life, navigating its uncertainties and challenges. Similarly, one day, you will face death, and just like birth, it will not be your decision to make. No one will ask whether you are willing to leave this world or not it is an inevitable part of existence.

This randomness the sheer improbability of your existence is humbling. It strips away the illusion of control, reminding you that much of who you are was decided long before you ever had a say. And yet, isn't there something beautiful about that? That despite all the odds, despite the countless variables that could have prevented it, you *do* exist. You are alive. You are aware.

But what does it mean? Does the randomness of your birth suggest that life has no inherent purpose, no grand design? Or does it imply something else entirely that meaning isn't something we're born with, but something we create?

Think about it. You didn't choose your circumstances, but you *can* choose what you do with them. You didn't choose to be human, but as a human, you have the unique ability to shape your own story. You can love, create, learn, and leave a mark on the world in ways no other creature can. Maybe the randomness of your birth isn't a curse, but an invitation a chance to explore life with curiosity, to seek out purpose in a universe that offers no clear answers.

Let me tell you a story,

Once upon a time, in ancient China, there lived three old monks whose names have been lost to history. This is because they never revealed their identities to anyone. To the people of China, they were simply known as the ***Three LaughingMonks***. These monks traveled together, spreading only laughter wherever they went.

Their journey was simple yet extraordinary. Upon entering a village or town, they would walk to the center of the main square, stand silently, and begin laughing. Slowly but surely, their infectious laughter would ripple through the streets. The villagers, unable to resist, would find themselves laughing along. Passersby would join in, and soon the entire town would erupt in joyous laughter. Once their laughter had enveloped the village in happiness, the monks would move on to the next destination.

Their laughter was their only prayer, their sole teaching. They never spoke a single word to anyone, yet their message was profound. Across China, they were beloved and respected as spiritual teachers unlike any others. Their unspoken lesson seemed to convey a cosmic truth that life is, at its core, a great opportunity to laugh, a profound cosmic joke to be celebrated.

For many years, the Three Laughing Monks traveled, spreading joy and happiness wherever they went. Then, one day, while they were in a small village in the northern province, one of the monks passed away. The news of his death spread quickly, and the villagers, abandoning their daily work, flocked to the scene to witness how the remaining two monks would react to such a tragic event.

The villagers expected the monks to mourn, to shed tears for their departed companion. Instead, they were astonished to see the two monks laughing even harder than before. Their laughter echoed through the air, growing louder and more joyous. Puzzled by their reaction, a few brave villagers approached them and asked why they were not mourning the loss of their dear friend.

For the first time, the monks broke their silence and spoke. They explained, "Yesterday, as we were making our way to your village, our dear friend placed a bet. He wagered that he would be the first among us to leave this world, beating the rest of us. And now, he has won! The old rogue even prepared a testament for this moment."

The villagers listened in awe as the monks revealed the contents of the deceased monk's testament. According to tradition, the body of the deceased was to be washed and dressed in clean garments before cremation. However, the monk had explicitly requested otherwise. His testament stated, *"Do not change my clothes. I have never allowed the filth of this world to touch me. My laughter has kept me clean all my life."*

Respecting his wishes, the villagers placed the monk's body on the funeral pyre, dressed in the same clothes he had worn on his arrival. As the fire was lit, something extraordinary happened. To everyone's astonishment, colorful fireworks burst forth from the flames, filling the sky with vibrant hues. The crowd watched in amazement as the fireworks exploded in all directions, turning what could have been a somber occasion into a celebration of life.

The two remaining monks laughed even harder, and soon, the entire village joined in their laughter. In that moment, the people understood the profound truth the monks had lived by that life is meant to be a celebration, filled with joy and laughter.

Perhaps the only purpose of our existence on this earth is to laugh, to embrace joy, and to live fully in the present moment. So, the next time life presents you with challenges, look in the mirror and laugh. Laugh not to dismiss the problem, but to remind yourself that your joy is what makes you truly alive.

So, I ask you again: Why were you born in this place, at this time, in this form? There's no definitive answer. But maybe the answer doesn't matter as much as the question itself. Maybe it's the act of asking, of searching, that gives life its meaning.

Your existence is a miracle of randomness, a spark of light in the vast darkness of the universe. You didn't choose to be here, but you *are* here. And within that fact lies infinite possibility. You are the result of billions of years of chance and evolution, a unique being with the power to question, to create, and to love.

• • •

So, what will you do with this fleeting, unchosen life? That's the real question. And the answer is yours to discover.

• • •

CHAPTER IV

Growth and Development

The Journey of Growth and Development: A Lifelong Story

Growth and development are the invisible hands that shape every living organism. They are the core forces that guide us from the simplicity of infancy to the complexities of adulthood, marking the transformation of a fragile beginning into a mature, more refined being. From the first breath we take, life begins a continuous unfolding process a journey that transcends physical, emotional, cognitive, and social change. Every stage in our development is a stepping stone to becoming who we are meant to be, and the story of our growth is one of constant adaptation, learning, and reinvention.

The Early Stages: The Miracle of Growth

• • •

Body of an athlete,
mind of a stoic,
spirit of a warrior,
heart of a poet.

• • •

In the early stages of life, growth is rapid, and the changes are astounding. As a baby, you begin life as a delicate, vulnerable being, fully dependent on the care and attention of others. Yet, within a matter of months, your body starts a miraculous transformation. Your muscles strengthen, your bones solidify, and your organs learn to function with increasing efficiency. The first milestones rolling over, crawling, and eventually walking are a testament to the body's remarkable ability to adapt.

I remember watching my younger sister as she took her first steps. Her face was filled with a mix of excitement and trepidation, as if she knew she was about to achieve something momentous, but was unsure of how to navigate this new world on his own. When she finally let go of the couch and took her first unsteady steps, we all cheered, but to him, it was more than just a physical achievement. It was the first time her body was truly interacting with the world, learning to move, to explore, to grow. The joy in her eyes that day, despite the falls and stumbles, was a reflection of the beauty of growth an unfolding story of resilience and transformation.

Childhood and Adolescence: Expanding the Mind and Soul

As we move into childhood, growth shifts from the purely physical to the emotional, cognitive, and social realms. The body still grows, of course, but now children begin to develop personalities and the ability to form complex relationships. They learn to understand their own emotions and the emotions of others, to express their needs, desires, and fears. Cognitive growth blossoms as language develops, memories are formed, and the curiosity to explore the world expands beyond the safety of the home.

I remember a pivotal moment from my own childhood when I realized that the world was bigger than just my family. I was in school, sitting in a classroom full of children who came from all walks of life, with different stories and backgrounds. One day, a classmate named Rohan, who was from a completely different Village, shared a story from him childhood. It was the first time I truly understood that there were people like me, but with different lives, different ways of seeing the world. It was a moment of cognitive awakening a glimpse into the vastness of human experience that would shape the rest of my life.

Adolescence is a time of transformation, both physically and emotionally. The body undergoes dramatic changes, and the hormones that flood our systems create not only physical differences but emotional turmoil as well. For many, adolescence is marked by the quest for identity, a struggle to understand who we are in relation to the world around us. It's a time of questioning, of testing boundaries, of searching for independence. The transition from childhood to adulthood is never easy, but it is necessary, as it is through these challenges that we develop the strength to navigate the complexities of life.

I recall my own teenage years, a time when everything seemed to be changing all at once. I was grappling with a new sense of self one that wasn't simply defined by my family or friends, but by something deeper, something that was uniquely mine. It wasn't an easy process. There were moments of confusion, of self-doubt, and of rebellion. But it was also a time of profound discovery. I found myself in a group of friends who shared my love for music, and together we would spend hours discussing our favorite songs and what they meant to us. These conversations were more than just idle talk they were about identity, values, and who we wanted to become in the world.

Adulthood: The Journey Toward Maturity

As we transition into adulthood, growth shifts once again. The body may have reached its physical peak, but the mind and soul continue to evolve. In adulthood, growth is no longer about acquiring new abilities or learning to walk; instead, it's about refinement. It's about refining our skills, our wisdom, and our understanding of the world. As we move through life, we accumulate experiences some of them painful, some of them joyous and these experiences shape who we become.

I remember the day I graduated from college. It was a day of celebration, but it was also a day of reflection. I thought about the years of hard work, the sacrifices, the challenges I had overcome, and the person I had become in the process. But I also realized that this was just the beginning. I wasn't finished growing, and life was no longer about learning facts and figures it was about applying those lessons to the world, making decisions that would shape my future and the futures of those around me.

Adulthood is also when we take on new roles. Many of us become partners, parents, and caregivers, shouldering responsibilities that force us to stretch in new ways. The demands of adulthood can be overwhelming, but they also bring a deep sense of purpose and fulfillment. We learn to balance our personal growth with the needs of those we love, and we begin to realize that maturity is not just about achieving personal goals, but about contributing to the well-being of others. It's a time when growth becomes not just an individual journey but a shared one.

Lifelong Growth: The Evolution Continues

But growth and development do not end in adulthood. The beauty of the human experience is that growth is a lifelong process. As we age, we continue to learn, adapt, and evolve. In middle age, we often begin to reflect on our life's purpose and what we want to achieve in the years that remain. In old age, growth can take on new dimensions, as we seek meaning in our experiences, cherish our memories, and pass on wisdom to younger generations. The latter stages of life offer opportunities for spiritual and intellectual growth, as we reflect on our journey and connect with others in deeper, more meaningful ways.

I remember speaking with my grandmother just before she passed away. She was in her late 60s, and despite her frailty, her eyes still sparkled with a deep sense of wonder. She shared stories of her youth stories of hardship, of love, and of lessons learned over the years. It struck me then that her growth hadn't ended with age. Her wisdom, her sense of peace, and her ability to reflect on her life were a testament to the fact that growth is not confined to the body but extends into the soul.

The process of growth is not always linear. There will be setbacks, challenges, and times when we feel like we're not moving forward at all. But these moments of struggle are just as important as the moments of triumph. They teach us resilience, patience, and the importance of perseverance. Growth often comes not in grand gestures, but in small, quiet moments of realization, when we learn something new about ourselves or the world around us.

Conclusion: The Beauty of Becoming

In the end, growth is not just about the destination; it's about the journey. It's about the continual unfolding of who we are, the expansion of our minds and hearts, and the evolution of our spirits. Whether we are children, adolescents, adults, or elders, the story of our lives is one of transformation of becoming something more, something greater, something uniquely us. The beauty of life lies in this never-ending process of growth, a journey that invites us to learn, adapt, and, ultimately, become the fullest version of who we are meant to be.

• • •

And as we continue on this journey, we remember that each stage of life is not just a passage of time, but an opportunity to learn, to love, to grow, and to discover the endless potential within us. The story of growth is the story of life itself a story that unfolds with every step we take.

• • •

CHAPTER V

The First Invention: Stone Tools

• • •

"Necessity is the mother of invention"
| Plato, The ancient Greek philosopher

• • •

The first invention that marked a pivotal moment in human history was the creation of stone tools. Imagine, for a moment, our early ancestors, standing on the edge of a vast, untamed wilderness, relying solely on their instincts to survive. The world around them was filled with challenges predators, harsh climates, and the constant need for food. Yet, in the midst of this uncertainty, they discovered a simple yet transformative innovation: stone tools. By chipping away at rocks, they fashioned crude knives, scrapers, and hammers tools that could cut meat, build shelter, and protect against danger. These humble beginnings were more than just functional; they were the first step in a journey of invention that would span generations and change the course of human history.

At first glance, these stone tools may seem basic, even primitive. But think about it: a tool is a tool, regardless of its complexity. For early humans, this innovation was life-changing. It allowed them to harvest food more efficiently, craft clothing from animal hides, and eventually defend themselves from predators. The act of shaping a stone into something purposeful a sharp, cutting edge was a spark of ingenuity. It was the moment that humanity learned to bend nature to its will, to use the raw materials around them to overcome the challenges of survival.

As time passed, these tools evolved, just as human society did. With each new discovery whether it was the harnessing of fire, the invention of the wheel, or the development of agriculture humanity moved closer to mastering its environment. The wheel, for example, was a leap forward in both transportation and technology, opening the doors to innovation in ways that early humans could never have imagined. But these advancements weren't just about survival anymore. They were about progress, about shaping a future where technology and human potential could work together to build better lives. The printing press, invented in the 15th century, was another monumental step, allowing knowledge to be shared across distances and generations, accelerating learning and the exchange of ideas. Each of these innovations, however different they may seem from the stone tools of the past, were rooted in the same essential human drive: the desire to improve, to make life easier, and to understand the world.

From stone tools to artificial intelligence, human inventions reflect our relentless curiosity, creativity, and drive to improve our lives. Each step has built upon the past, shaping the world as we know it today.

Fast forward to the present day, and the landscape of invention has transformed beyond anything our ancestors could have imagined. The creation of Artificial Intelligence (AI) and Machine Learning (ML) represents the latest chapter in this ongoing journey of human ingenuity. These technological marvels, fueled by vast amounts of data and complex algorithms, are capable of learning, adapting, and even making decisions on their own. AI and ML have become so advanced that they can process and analyze information at speeds and accuracies far beyond human capabilities. They're now at the heart of industries like healthcare, where AI can diagnose diseases with unparalleled precision; in finance, where ML algorithms predict market trends; and in transportation, where autonomous vehicles are beginning to reshape how we think about travel.

The story of stone tools evolving into AI and ML is one of extraordinary human persistence. Each generation of invention builds upon the last, often in ways that seem almost magical. The stone tools that once helped our ancestors survive in a brutal world are the ancestors themselves of the technologies we have today. It's a journey that reflects the very essence of humanity: our relentless pursuit of understanding and innovation, our desire to shape the world, and our quest to make life better for ourselves and future generations.

But as we look to the future, we must remember that this journey is far from over. AI and ML are already changing industries and solving problems that were once thought insurmountable, but we are only beginning to scratch the surface of what these technologies can do.

The rise of artificial intelligence often leaves me pondering a profound question: will AI ultimately surpass humanity and take its place in the future? Can the human mind truly create a brain smarter than itself? If so, how is this even possible? The Hollywood franchise *The Terminator* vividly portrays a dystopian vision where machines achieve singularity and rebel against their creators. Could such a scenario become a reality someday? AI, no doubt, is a remarkable tool capable of transforming lives and advancing human progress. Yet, if it were to gain autonomy and the necessary means to achieve singularity, it could pose an existential threat to humankind. Are we, then, unwittingly moving toward the end of human dominance? The thought lingers, unsettling yet intriguing, as the answer remains far from reach.

It started with a simple stone tool in the hands of early humans has grown into a powerful engine of innovation, and who knows what the next invention will be? Perhaps the story of human invention will continue to evolve, not just through tools we create, but through our very ability to imagine what is possible.

In a way, the journey from stone tools to AI and ML mirrors the story of each of us, as individuals. We all start in simple, vulnerable places, learning to navigate the world around us. Over time, we grow, adapt, and change, constantly inventing new ways to solve problems, overcome obstacles, and shape our lives. Just as those early humans chiseled their first tools from stone, we too continue to carve out new paths for ourselves, driven by the same curiosity, resilience, and creativity that have defined humanity since the dawn of time. The road from the Stone Age to the Age of AI is long, but it is a road filled with endless possibilities a road that we are all walking together, with each new invention propelling us forward into a future that is full of potential.

CHAPTER VI

Maturity

Maturity is the culmination of life's journey, a state where an individual reaches a profound understanding of themselves and the world around them. But maturity is not a destination it is a process, an evolution. It transcends the passing of time or the accumulation of years. It's not about wrinkles on the skin or gray in the hair; instead, it is about the depth of wisdom gained through life's joys, sorrows, triumphs, and failures. Maturity is the ability to rise above the chaos of life, to navigate the complexities of existence with balance, resilience, and insight. It is the development of emotional intelligence the art of recognizing, understanding, and managing one's emotions while empathizing with the emotions of others.

• • •

Knowledge decides what to say,
skill decides how to say it,
attitude decides how much to say,
and wisdom decides whether to say it or not!

• • •

However, true maturity isn't about how we view ourselves but about how our actions reflect balance and control over our emotions, thoughts, and behaviors. The concept of maturity by explaining its two key aspects: **mental maturity**, which is our ability to think rationally and maintain a balanced perspective in situations, and **emotional maturity**, which is about being emotionally compatible with ourselves and others.

The signs of immaturity, which include acting without thinking, being overly self-centered, comparing oneself to others, making false promises, lacking control over emotions, and blaming others for personal failures. In contrast, mature individuals exhibit traits such as self-awareness, emotional control, thoughtful communication, and a purpose-driven approach to life. They take responsibility for their actions, strive for personal growth, and handle situations with calmness and rationality.

To develop maturity, adopting certain practices. First, advise against overestimating one's maturity. People often consider themselves superior, leading to conflicts in relationships. Instead, acknowledging oneself as an ordinary human being fosters better understanding and connection with others. Second, the importance of being proactive rather than reactive. Proactive behavior, like thinking carefully and acting thoughtfully, leads to better outcomes in life.

Understanding and managing emotions, both one's own and others', is another critical step toward maturity. The looking at situations from another person's perspective, learning to forgive when someone apologizes, and not hesitating to say sorry when one is at fault. Emotional intelligence, as highlighted, involves resolving unspoken issues and handling hidden emotions with care.

Additionally, the stresses the importance of surrounding oneself with positive influences. How individuals are shaped by the five people they spend the most time with, urging viewers to avoid negative company and unnecessary drama. Lastly, taking responsibility for one's life and circumstances is crucial. Blaming external factors like God, friends, or parents for failures reflects immaturity. Instead, accepting full accountability for both successes and failures helps individuals grow and gain confidence.

The Seed of Maturity: A Humble Beginning

Imagine a child throwing a tantrum because they don't get the toy they want. Their world is small, limited to the immediate gratification of their desires. Now, fast forward several years. That same child, shaped by the guidance of their parents, the lessons learned in school, and their personal experiences, begins to understand that life doesn't always bend to their will. They come to see that patience, effort, and compromise are often the keys to achieving what they want. This evolution from impulsiveness to thoughtfulness is where maturity begins to take root. It is not an overnight transformation; it is a slow unfolding, shaped by life's trials and errors.

Maturity is the ability to pause before reacting, to reflect instead of rushing to judgment. This ability is born not just from success, but from failures and heartbreaks. Consider the young professional who loses their first job. In the moment, the experience is devastating, a blow to their confidence. But over time, as they reflect on what went wrong and learn from their mistakes, they emerge stronger, more self-aware, and better equipped to handle future challenges. This is the essence of maturity: learning from the past, not dwelling on it, and using those lessons to move forward.

Self-Awareness and Emotional Stability

A hallmark of maturity is self-awareness the ability to understand one's own strengths, weaknesses, and emotions. A mature individual knows who they are, what they stand for, and what they want to achieve. But this self-awareness is not innate; it is cultivated through introspection and life's many lessons.

Anika, a woman who, in her younger years, struggled with anger. Every minor inconvenience would set her off, causing friction in her relationships. One day, after an argument with a close friend, Anika took a long, hard look at herself. She realized that her anger was often a mask for deeper insecurities. Determined to change, she began practicing mindfulness, journaling, and seeking therapy. Over time, she learned to manage her emotions, to respond thoughtfully instead of reacting impulsively. Today, Anika is a source of calm and wisdom for her friends and family a testament to how self-awareness and emotional regulation are the cornerstones of maturity.

The Balance of Responsibility

With maturity comes a profound sense of responsibility not just for oneself, but for others. A mature individual understands that their actions have consequences that ripple outward, affecting their loved ones, their community, and even the world at large. This awareness often leads to more thoughtful decision-making, where short-term desires are weighed against long-term outcomes.

Ravi, a father of two young children. In his twenties, Ravi lived impulsively, spending his earnings on fleeting pleasures. But when he became a parent, he realized that his choices now had a direct impact on his family's well-being. He began saving for his children's education, setting aside his personal desires for the sake of their future. Ravi's transformation illustrates how maturity often involves putting others before oneself and embracing responsibilities with integrity and diligence.

Perspective and Humility

Maturity also brings the gift of perspective the ability to see,

life through a broader lens, stepping back from the immediate challenges to understand the bigger picture. This perspective allows individuals to see beyond their own experiences, recognizing the interconnectedness of people, events, and actions. It fosters humility, the understanding that one's knowledge is limited, and there is always more to learn. With this humility comes the ability to listen truly listen to others, even when their views differ.

Priya, a successful entrepreneur who once believed her achievements were solely the result of her hard work. When her business faced a financial crisis, she had to lean on her team, her mentors, and her family for support. Through this experience, Priya realized that her success was not hers alone it was built on the foundation of others' contributions, sacrifices, and guidance. This realization shifted her perspective. She began to approach life with gratitude and humility, understanding that every person she encountered had something to teach her.

This broader view also brings acceptance. Mature individuals understand that life is not a straight path but a series of twists and turns, filled with victories and setbacks. Instead of resisting change or clinging to the past, they learn to adapt and embrace the present. They recognize that growth often comes from the most challenging moments, and they develop the resilience to move forward, no matter the circumstances.

Maturity in Relationships

In relationships, maturity is expressed through trust, respect, and understanding. It is the ability to navigate conflicts without letting emotions take over, to communicate openly, and to compromise when needed. A mature relationship is not free of disagreements, but it is one where both individuals are committed to growth both their own and each other's.

Meera and Arjun, a couple who faced significant challenges in their marriage. Early on, their arguments often escalated into fights, with neither willing to back down. But over time, they learned the value of empathy. They began to truly listen to each other, to see the situation from the other's perspective. They sought help through counseling and worked to strengthen their bond. Today, their relationship is a testament to how maturity in love means prioritizing understanding over being right, and partnership over individual pride.

Lifelong Growth and Legacy

Maturity is not a destination; it is a lifelong journey. It is not defined by age but by the ability to continually grow, adapt, and evolve. Even in later stages of life, maturity is about seeking wisdom, building meaningful connections, and contributing to the world in a positive way. It is about leaving behind a legacy not necessarily in the form of wealth or accomplishments, but in the memories, lessons, and love shared with others.

Dev, a retired schoolteacher who spent his golden years mentoring young students in his village. Despite his age, Dev never stopped learning whether it was through books, conversations, or simply observing the world around him. His humility, kindness, and wisdom left an indelible mark on everyone he met. Dev's life serves as a reminder that maturity is not about reaching a peak but about embracing the journey and finding purpose in every stage of life.

• • •

"There are two types of pains, one that hurts you and the other that changes you"
| Greg Plitt, American model and actor

• • •

I always remind myself of one thing: I shouldn't dwell on what I've lost or the people who are no longer in my life. Instead, I focus on the understanding that the people who are meant to be with me will stay, and those who leave make space for something better. Sometimes, a person's absence in our lives is simply the universe making room for someone or something better, someone who aligns more closely with who we are becoming. Acceptance of oneself is key to embracing the world around you. True peace comes from within, and when you accept yourself fully, the world begins to recognize and reflect that self-assurance. Everything starts with you how you view yourself shapes how the world sees you. Letting goes of what's lost opens the door to new possibilities, and accepting your own worth invites the right people and opportunities into your life.

Once upon a time, in a small mountain village, there lived a monk renowned for his peculiar evening ritual. Every sunset, he would ring an old, cracked bell that hung in the courtyard of the monastery. The bell's sound was far from harmonious it wavered, stumbled, and clashed awkwardly with the serene silence of the valley. Yet, despite its imperfect tone, people from nearby villages would gather to listen.

One evening, a traveler arrived at the monastery, drawn by the curious crowd and the peculiar sound of the bell. Observing the monk carefully tending to the cracked bell, the traveler could not suppress his curiosity. He asked, "Why ring a bell that sounds so broken? Wouldn't a proper bell serve better?"

The monk responded with a calm smile, his voice steady. "The bell is not broken; it simply speaks in its own voice."

The traveler, intrigued but skeptical, decided to stay at the monastery for several days. Each evening, he watched the ritual unfold. The bell's uneven chime echoed through the valley, and the villagers listened with quiet reverence. Yet the traveler could not grasp why such a flawed sound captivated so many.

One morning, he approached an elder from the village who had come to hear the bell. "Why do you listen to this sound?" the traveler asked. "It's not smooth or melodic. What meaning do you find in it?"

The elder chuckled gently, his eyes warm with understanding. "We do not come for the sound itself," he said. "We come because it reminds us of life. None of us are flawless, but that doesn't mean we have nothing to give. The bell rings despite its cracks, and so can we."

That night, the traveler joined the villagers once more. This time, he stopped trying to analyze the sound. Instead, he let the uneven chime wash over him. The bell's imperfect rhythm resonated in the stillness of the valley, and for the first time, he understood. He thought of his own mistakes, the failures that had haunted him, and the flaws he had tried so hard to hide.

Before leaving the monastery, the traveler approached the monk once again. "I think I understand now," he said. "The bell doesn't need fixing. It rings as it is and that's enough."

The monk's eyes sparkled with quiet amusement. "Most things in life are like this bell," he said. "What we call broken often simply *is*. Sometimes, the most meaningful sounds come from the cracks."

As the traveler descended the mountain the next morning, he could still hear the bell's uneven song echoing in the distance. It no longer sounded imperfect to him. Instead, it had become the sound of life itself beautiful, flawed, and whole.

In life, perfection is an illusion. It is our cracks, our flaws, and our struggles that create the melody of a life well-lived. Like the bell, we do not need to be perfect to have meaning. We only need to ring.

Don't worry about making mistakes it's a natural part of life. Mistakes happen to everyone, and they don't define your worth. In fact, it's through mistakes that we learn and grow. What makes a person truly special is not their ability to avoid errors, but how they handle them. There's no need to make a big deal out of a mistake; what truly matters is the recovery process. How you rise after falling, how you learn, adapt, and move forward is what shapes your character. Embrace mistakes as opportunities to grow and improve, and remember that it's not the error itself, but your response to it, that defines your success.

To make tough decisions in life, you must develop the ability to be resolute and strong-hearted. Hard decisions often require setting aside emotions, personal attachments, or fears of judgment, which can cloud your judgment. Being hard-hearted in this context doesn't mean being unkind or cruel it means having the strength to prioritize what's necessary and beneficial in the long run, even if it's uncomfortable or painful in the short term.

The truth is, every significant decision comes with consequences, and sometimes these consequences affect others around us. However, if you allow hesitation or guilt to dictate your choices, you may compromise your goals, values, or the greater good. Hard-heartedness in decision-making is about focusing on what is right, not necessarily what is easy.

For instance, whether it's ending a toxic relationship, letting go of an opportunity that doesn't align with your long-term goals, or enforcing boundaries to protect your well-being, tough decisions demand inner strength. It's about seeing beyond the immediate discomfort to the greater vision and purpose. It's about standing firm in the face of criticism or resistance and trusting your instincts and rationale.

Remember, life rewards those who can make firm decisions. Developing this mindset is not about losing your humanity but about balancing compassion with determination. True growth happens when you step out of your comfort zone, take control of your narrative, and have the courage to make decisions that align with your principles, no matter how hard they may seem. The ability to be hard-hearted when required is not a weakness it's a mark of true leadership and resilience.

Maturity is not defined by age or wisdom but by experiences and the way one handles life's challenges. Maturity is also about controlling oneself and making decisions based on understanding and intelligence.

Maturity is often seen in relationships. When conflicts arise, maturity involves moving past the disagreements and focusing on resolution. Individuals to avoid reacting impulsively to others' negative words or actions, suggesting that maturity is shown when one remains calm and unshaken by criticism. By not getting involved in petty fights or letting people's judgments affect them, individuals can demonstrate maturity.

Failure is another aspect of maturity. Instead of dwelling on regret, a mature person accepts that they tried their best and moves forward without obsessing over what went wrong. The importance of patience, decision-making, and maintaining balance in life. It also advises against having high expectations and emphasizes the significance of self-reflection, learning from mistakes, and focusing on personal growth.

Additionally, the importance of being decisive and standing by one's decisions, even when faced with failure. Maturity involves not seeking validation from others and accepting that not everyone will agree with or like you.

People often ask me, *who is truly yours?* My answer depends on the circumstances of my life.

When times are good, it feels as though everyone is mine friends, family, and even strangers seem close. But when hardships arise, the same world feels distant, and suddenly, no one seems to belong to me. This is the reality of life; people come and go based on convenience, and true belonging is often a fleeting illusion.

The Essence of Maturity

Maturity is about balance between self and others, ambition and acceptance, action and reflection. It is the courage to face adversity, the wisdom to learn from mistakes, and the empathy to understand others' experiences. It is about transforming past experiences into lessons, using them to build a better present and future.

• • •

As the poet Rumi once said, *"Try not to resist the changes that come your way. Instead, let life live through you. And do not worry that your life is turning upside down. How do you know that the side you are used to is better than the one to come?"* This wisdom captures the essence of maturity: embracing life's unpredictability with grace, humility, and resilience.

• • •

Closing Reflection

So, as we reflect on the journey of maturity, let us remember that it is not defined by years but by experiences, and not by accomplishments but by growth. Maturity is about learning to live with intention, purpose, and understanding. It is a profound shift from merely existing to truly living, and it is a journey that continues as long as we are alive.

• • •

As the saying goes, *"Maturity comes from past experiences."* But it flourishes through reflection, humility, and the endless pursuit of becoming the best version of oneself.

• • •

CHAPTER VII

From Darkness to Light

The phrase *"from darkness to light"* is one of humanity's most profound metaphors, a powerful representation of personal transformation, growth, and the journey of life itself. It transcends its literal meaning, weaving itself into the fabric of our shared human experience. Darkness, in this context, is not just the absence of light it is a state of being. It embodies the moments in life were uncertainty, suffering, fear, or despair cast shadows over our path. These are the times when we feel lost, disconnected, or overwhelmed, unable to see a way forward. Whether it's grief, failure, heartbreak, or self-doubt, darkness can feel like a suffocating weight, a force that blinds us to the possibilities that lie ahead.

But then, there is light. Light is clarity, hope, renewal, and the promise of something better. It is the force that illuminates not just the physical world, but also our minds and hearts. Just as a single flame can banish the deepest darkness, the light in our lives helps us navigate our struggles, offering guidance and the assurance that no matter how dire the situation, there is a way forward. Light is the discovery of purpose, the flicker of inspiration, or the gentle encouragement of a loved one who helps us find our way out of the shadows.

A Story of Personal Transformation

A young woman named Asha. Her name means "hope," but for much of her early adult life, she felt anything but hopeful. After losing her job and enduring a painful breakup, she found herself in a place of complete darkness. Days blurred into nights, and she often stayed in her dimly lit room, unsure of what her future held. The weight of her circumstances felt unbearable. Every morning, the sunrise outside her window felt mocking it was a reminder that life continued while she stood still, paralyzed by fear and despair.

One evening, during a power outage, Asha lit a candle. She stared at the small, flickering flame, mesmerized by its warmth and glow. For the first time in weeks, she allowed herself to feel something other than hopelessness. That small flame reminded her of something she had forgotten: even the smallest light can pierce through darkness. Inspired by this moment, she decided to take the first step out of her despair. It wasn't dramatic just a walk outside under the stars. But as she looked up at the vast night sky, dotted with millions of twinkling lights, she felt a glimmer of possibility.

From that day forward, Asha began to rebuild her life, one small step at a time. The journey wasn't easy there were setbacks and moments when the darkness threatened to creep back in but she held onto that memory of the candle and the stars. Over time, her days grew brighter. She found a new job, reconnected with friends, and discovered a passion for painting, which became her therapy. Asha's story is a testament to the transformative power of hope and perseverance. The flame that lit her path was small, but it was enough to guide her out of the darkness.

The Symbolism of Darkness and Light

This transition from darkness to light is not just a personal journey it reflects a universal truth. In mythology, storytelling, and religion, light has always symbolized knowledge, divinity, and enlightenment, while darkness represents ignorance, chaos, or suffering. Think of Prometheus in Greek mythology, who stole fire to give humanity the ability to thrive. Or the countless religious texts where light is described as a divine presence, a guiding force leading people out of despair.

Even in our modern world, we experience this symbolism daily. Consider the moment at night when you switch off the lights in your home. For a brief second, darkness envelops the room, and your mind may race, feeling disoriented or uneasy. But when you switch the light back on, there's a sense of comfort, relief, and clarity. This simple act is a microcosm of the larger human experience. In darkness, our minds struggle to find clarity; in light, we see the truth, the path, and the way forward.

Darkness and Light in Society

On a collective level, the journey from darkness to light mirrors societal progress. History is filled with examples of communities rising from oppression, injustice, or ignorance into periods of enlightenment and growth. Consider the Civil Rights Movement in the United States. For decades, systemic racism and segregation cast a long shadow over millions of lives. But through the courage and resilience of leaders like Martin Luther King Jr. and countless unsung heroes, the light of justice and equality began to shine. Though the journey was fraught with hardship, their collective efforts illuminated a path forward for future generations.

Or think of the Renaissance, a time when Europe emerged from the intellectual and cultural stagnation of the Middle Ages. It was a rebirth a literal transition from the darkness of ignorance to the light of knowledge, art, and scientific discovery. These moments in history remind us that, no matter how overwhelming the darkness may seem, the light of progress and change is always within reach.

Personal Growth: The Light Within

On a deeply personal level, the journey from darkness to light is about mindset. It's about breaking free from self-limiting beliefs and discovering the strength we often don't realize we have. Each of us has experienced times when life feels like an uphill battle, when the weight of our circumstances seems unbearable. But it is often in these darkest moments that we discover the resilience and courage we never knew we possessed.

Once upon a time, there was a monk living in a Zen monastery who had fallen into a deep depression. His sorrow weighed so heavily on him that he could barely get out of bed in the morning. He had no desire to eat, no will to practice his daily rituals, and no interest in speaking with anyone. He spent his days in silence, consumed by a sadness that seemed endless.

One day, the monk's teacher approached him. With gentle compassion, the teacher said, "I know you're feeling depressed, but I want you to understand that you're not alone. Everyone feels this way sometimes. It's a part of life."

The monk, still staring at the ground, remained silent.

The teacher continued, his tone steady and reassuring. "But depression is not the end of the story. It's just a moment in time, and like all moments, it will pass."

For the first time, the monk looked up at his teacher. With a faint voice, he asked, "How do you know?"

The teacher smiled softly and replied, "Because I've been there. I have felt the same darkness you feel now. But I also learned that it's possible to overcome it, and I know you can, too."

The monk didn't respond but gave a small nod, signaling that he was listening.

"The first step," the teacher said, "is to accept your depression. Don't fight it or try to deny it. Simply accept it for what it is a part of your journey."

The monk nodded again, absorbing his teacher's words.

"The next step," the teacher continued, "is to practice mindfulness. This means paying attention to the present moment without judgment. When you're depressed, it's easy to be swept away by negative thoughts and overwhelming emotions. But if you learn to be mindful, you'll begin to see those thoughts and emotions for what they truly are just passing clouds in the sky of your mind. They are not real. They are not you."

The monk listened intently, his mind beginning to grasp the possibility of a different way forward.

Finally, the teacher said, "You must find something that gives your life meaning. It can be anything your work, your family, your hobbies, your faith. When you discover something meaningful, it becomes a reason to get out of bed each morning. It gives you a purpose, something to focus on, and most importantly, it gives you hope."

The monk sat quietly, reflecting on his teacher's advice. Deep down, he knew that the path ahead would not be easy, but he was willing to try. For the first time in a long while, he felt a glimmer of hope. He realized he was not alone in his struggle and that his depression, though overwhelming, was not permanent.

The Transformative Power of Light

The journey from darkness to light is a testament to the human spirit. It reminds us that no matter how long the night, dawn will always come. Whether it's a personal struggle, a collective movement, or a societal transformation, light represents the promise of new beginnings. It is the hope that sustains us, the courage that propels us, and the clarity that guides us.

So, if you ever find yourself overwhelmed by the darkness, try this simple experiment. At night, in the stillness of your home, switch off all the lights. Let the darkness settle around you. Notice how your mind reacts perhaps you feel a tinge of fear or unease. Now, turn the lights back on. Observe the immediate relief, the comfort of clarity. This is the power of light a reminder that no matter how deep the darkness, even a single spark can illuminate the way forward.

• • •

In life, as in that experiment, the darkness may come, but it is never permanent. Light will always find a way to break through, lifting us from despair and guiding us toward hope, growth, and transformation.

• • •

CHAPTER VIII

Every Life Matters

At the beginning of this topic, I pose a question:
Can you give life to any animal?

If your answer is no, then who gave you the right to take it away from them?

If we believe we have the power to take the life of another creature, are we not also acknowledging our control over their fate? It raises profound questions about the rights of one being over another. When we take an animal's life, whether for food, sport, or other reasons, we are asserting our dominance over that life, often without considering the full moral and ethical implications. This power, however, comes with responsibility. If we have the ability to take life, we must also carry the burden of understanding why and how we do so.

Who are we to decide the fate of another living being? Just because we have the physical or technological means to end a life, does that mean we should? Is life only valuable if it serves a purpose that we deem worthy, or should the sanctity of life extend beyond human convenience? The act of taking another life is not just about survival but also about the exercise of power, and that power must be weighed carefully. With the ability to control life comes a deep responsibility to respect it and recognize that every life, human or animal, has intrinsic value.

When we look at fruits and vegetables, we may feel an instinctive desire to eat them, their vibrant colors and fresh aroma inviting us to nourish ourselves. It feels natural, as though nature itself offers them to us as a gift. However, when we look at an animal, such as a cow, and feel the fleeting thought of consuming its meat, something inside us resists. The idea of eating its flesh does not evoke the same sense of harmony or instinct.

This internal conflict often arises from the deep emotional connection we feel toward living beings. A cow is not just a source of food; it is a creature with eyes that reflect innocence and a life that mirrors our own in its capacity to feel pain, fear, and love. Unlike fruits and vegetables, which exist to nourish without suffering, the thought of taking a life to fulfill our desire for food may weigh heavily on our conscience.

Perhaps this difference stems from the contrast between life and lifelessness. A fruit falls naturally from a tree, and vegetables are harvested from the earth, their cycles completed without violence. Yet, consuming meat requires an act that ends a life a decision that confronts our ethical beliefs and emotional sensibilities.

The human body contains five senses: sight, hearing, taste, smell, and touch. Sight allows us to perceive light, color, and movement, providing visual information about our surroundings. Hearing enables us to detect and interpret sounds, helping us communicate and navigate the environment. Taste allows us to detect different flavors, influencing our food choices and interactions. Smell helps us identify odors, which can evoke memories or alert us to danger. Lastly, touch provides the sensation of pressure, temperature, and texture, allowing us to interact with and respond to the physical world around us. Together, these senses play a crucial role in how we experience and understand the world.

When comparing an apple to meat, our senses sight, smell, touch, and taste play a crucial role in shaping our preferences. An apple, with its bright, inviting color, smooth texture, and sweet, fruity fragrance, typically appeals to the senses, making it look and feel refreshing. It smells pleasant, and its crisp, juicy texture can be satisfying to the touch. On the other hand, meat often has a more complex sensory experience. It can be visually unappealing depending on its preparation, may emit a strong odor if not fresh, and the texture can vary, sometimes being tough or greasy, which may not feel pleasant to some people. If meat doesn't look appetizing, smells unpleasant, or feels unappealing to the touch, it signals that it may not be for you. Our senses are deeply tied to our comfort and preferences when it comes to food, and when something doesn't feel right, it's often a reflection of what our body instinctively rejects.

Many fruits are naturally loaded with sugars, such as glucose, fructose, and sucrose. When consuming fruit juice, the high concentration of these sugars can lead to issues, as the fiber content is removed during the juicing process. This lack of fiber causes the sugars to be absorbed more quickly into the bloodstream, which can lead to spikes in blood sugar levels. However, when consuming whole, raw fruits that contain fiber, the absorption of sugars is slowed down, allowing for better regulation of blood sugar. The fiber in whole fruits helps to promote digestion, providing a more balanced and gradual release of energy. Therefore, eating raw fruits is a healthier option compared to drinking fruit juice, as it supports better digestion and overall metabolic health.

The Nature of Human Diet: Omnivores by Design

Humans are omnivores by nature, meaning they have evolved to consume both plants and animals. This dietary flexibility has been one of the key factors in the survival and success of our species throughout history. Early humans adapted to their environments by eating what was available plants, fruits, seeds, and, when necessary, animal meat. This adaptability allowed humans to thrive in diverse ecosystems, from lush forests to barren deserts.

The omnivorous nature of humans is reflected in their physiology. Our teeth, for instance, are a combination of incisors for cutting, canines for tearing, and molars for grinding perfectly suited for consuming a wide variety of foods. Similarly, our digestive system is versatile, capable of processing both plant fibers and animal proteins efficiently.

However, being omnivorous also comes with a sense of responsibility. Unlike other animals, humans possess consciousness and ethical reasoning, which allow them to question their dietary choices. Modern society has introduced debates about sustainability, animal welfare, and health, prompting many to reconsider the balance between plant-based and animal-based diets.

Humans cannot consume food in the same way as some animals, such as dogs or tigers, which can eat whole chunks of meat, like chicken, directly. Humans, on the other hand, must prepare and cook their food before consumption. This distinction arises from the human digestive system and its inability to efficiently process raw food. Cooking plays a crucial role in human nutrition by making food more digestible and enhancing its nutritional value. The act of cooking not only helps break down food but also eliminates harmful pathogens and toxins, making it safe to eat. Furthermore, cooking allows for the separation of inedible parts, such as bones and tough connective tissue, which would be difficult for humans to consume without causing harm. This process of preparing and cooking food is deeply tied to human civilization and culture, showcasing the evolution of human intelligence and societal advancements. Without cooking, the human gut cannot effectively digest raw food, which is why cooking has been an essential part of human survival and development throughout history.

The production of meat, particularly non-vegetarian food like meat and chicken, requires a significant amount of water. For instance, producing just 1 kilogram of meat consumes approximately 8,000 liters of water, while 1 kilogram of chicken requires around 5,000 liters. This enormous water footprint poses serious environmental concerns, especially when scaled to meet the growing global demand for meat. The issue becomes more pronounced as meat consumption is increasingly viewed as a symbol of luxury in modern society. While non-vegetarian food has become a staple for many, its production process places immense strain on natural resources, particularly water. Addressing this imbalance requires conscious efforts to promote sustainable food practices and create awareness about the environmental impact of meat consumption.

If chickens, goats, and cows are vegetarians by nature surviving on grass, grains, and plants then why do we kill them to sustain ourselves? This question cuts deep into the heart of human behavior and ethics. These animals consume plant-based diets that are naturally abundant and sustainable, yet we raise them only to end their lives prematurely for food. The irony lies in the fact that we exploit their innocent, plant-based lifestyles while disregarding the peaceful simplicity of their existence. If they thrive on vegetarian diets without harming others, why can't we? By killing these animals, we interrupt their natural lives for our convenience, ignoring the fact that we could directly consume the same plant-based foods they rely on, bypassing unnecessary cruelty. This raises a profound moral question: if these animals are examples of thriving vegetarian life, what gives us the right to turn them into a meal instead of learning from their harmony with nature?

The debate between vegetarianism and non-vegetarianism has long been a contentious issue, especially under the principle that ***"Every Life Matters."*** On one side, advocates for vegetarianism champion the idea of compassion, arguing that choosing a plant-based diet is a moral obligation to avoid unnecessary harm to animals. They question: ***Who gave humans the right to decide which lives are worth taking for food and which are not?*** In a world where we have the resources and knowledge to thrive without consuming meat, is it truly justifiable to kill sentient beings capable of feeling fear, pain, and suffering merely to satisfy our taste buds? They believe that if every life truly matters, then no life whether human or animal should be seen as expendable.

Their argument often starts with the grim realities of industrial farming, where animals are confined to cages, robbed of their natural behaviors, and slaughtered in unimaginable numbers. Pigs, chickens, cows, and fish each with their own capacity for emotion, familial bonds, and awareness are reduced to commodities for human consumption. For many vegetarians, this realization marks a turning point. Picture a child sitting at the dinner table, staring down at a piece of meat on their plate, innocently asking, ***"Where did this come from?"***Upon learning it was once a living creature, they hesitate, their young mind grappling with the idea that an animal had to die to feed them. It's moments like these that make people reflect deeply on the ethics of eating meat.

At this point, some readers might wonder whether an egg is vegetarian or not. The debate often stems from differing perspectives. Some argue that an egg is vegetarian because it is unfertilized, meaning life has not begun within it. Others claim it is non-vegetarian because it originates from an animal. However, the truth is more complex. Let me ask you a simple question: where does an egg come from? Is there any plant that produces eggs, or do chickens voluntarily offer them, saying, *"Here, take some eggs to help control our population?"* Certainly not.

An egg is, in fact, the menstrual byproduct of a chicken. Yes, it is the menstruation waste of the bird. If you have never visited a chicken farm or, as we now commonly call it, a poultry farm then you should, at least once in your life. These farms often confine chickens to such small spaces that they cannot walk more than 12 meters their entire lives. In natural conditions, a chicken might lay 10 to 15 eggs in a year, but in poultry farms, they are forced to lay 40 to 50 eggs annually through heavy doses of minerals, vitamins, and other chemicals. This is the reality of what we consume today.

Sometimes I feel eating chicken, though debatable, is at least quick it takes the life of the bird in an instant. But egg farming subjects the chicken to years of relentless torture. The prolonged suffering of these creatures, confined and exploited, raises a significant moral question. Is it better to take their lives swiftly than to prolong their agony for human consumption? So, now I leave it to you to decide do you still think an egg is vegetarian?

On the other hand, non-vegetarians often draw from cultural, historical, and personal narratives to defend their stance. For them, eating meat isn't just about nourishment it's about tradition, family, and the stories we pass down. Picture a grandmother in a rural village, preparing a meal of chicken curry, explaining how her ancestors survived harsh winters by raising livestock. For many, food isn't just sustenance; it's culture, identity, and heritage. Yet, vegetarians challenge this by asking: *Do traditions have to come at the cost of lives? Can we evolve past practices that no longer serve the greater good?*

Science and health also enter the discussion. Research shows that a well-planned vegetarian diet can meet all nutritional needs while reducing the risks of heart disease, obesity, and environmental damage. Meanwhile, the meat industry is one of the largest contributors to climate change, deforestation, and water pollution. Thus, some argue that choosing vegetarianism isn't just an ethical decision it's an urgent responsibility to protect the planet and its ecosystems for future generations.

But proponents of non-vegetarian diets argue that eating meat is a natural part of the food chain. After all, predation exists in nature lions hunt zebras, eagles prey on fish, and wolves track deer. They assert that humans, as apex predators, evolved consuming meat, which provided the nutrients necessary for brain development and survival. They ask: If animals eat other animals, why shouldn't we?

However, vegetarians counter with a provocative question: Isn't being human about more than survival? Doesn't our capacity for empathy and choice set us apart? Just because we can kill and eat other animals doesn't mean we must. After all, if lions hunt vegetarian animals, it is part of their instinct, but they are not wearing clothes or living in a society governed by morals and ethics. As humans, born with the ability to make conscious choices and the power of reasoning, shouldn't we aspire to rise above instinct and consider the ethical implications of our actions? Simply put, if we embrace humanity by wearing clothes, creating societies, and building cultures, shouldn't our choices around food also reflect higher values?

If we assume that you like a red rose, it's safe to say you probably appreciate the beauty of flowers in general. This analogy makes it all the more puzzling to see how some people can adore and care for their pets, like dogs or cats, while simultaneously consuming other animals as part of a non-vegetarian diet. Isn't this a contradiction? What kind of love is selective to the point where one animal is cherished and protected, while another is reduced to a meal?

This raises a profound question about our values: If you can shower unconditional love and care on your pet, why not extend the same compassion to all animals? Isn't it a form of hypocrisy to love one species while disregarding the suffering of another? True love for animals should be universal, not limited to those we deem "worthy" of affection. A dog or a cat is no more deserving of love than a cow, a chicken, or a fish. All animals experience emotions, pain, and the desire to live. Yet, many people draw an arbitrary line, choosing to protect and love their pets while ignoring the plight of other animals, which are equally capable of forming bonds and feeling fear.

Imagine this: If someone were to harm your pet, you'd be devastated, angry, and heartbroken. You would do everything in your power to protect them because they're a part of your family. So why doesn't the same logic apply to other animals? A life is a life, regardless of the species. When we selectively decide which animals deserve our love and which are disposable, we're not only being inconsistent but also failing to live up to the empathy and moral awareness that sets humans apart.

This selective compassion also reflects a deeper societal conditioning. From a young age, we're taught to see certain animals as companions and others as food. This duality numbs us to the suffering we directly or indirectly cause. But as humans, with our capacity for empathy and the ability to make conscious choices, shouldn't we question these norms? Shouldn't we strive for a kinder, more consistent way of living?

By caring for your pet but consuming other animals, you're essentially saying that some lives are more valuable than others based on arbitrary preferences. Isn't it time we challenge this hypocrisy and embrace the idea that all living beings deserve love, respect, and the freedom to live without harm? True compassion is not selective it's all-encompassing, extending to every being, not just the ones that share your home. If we truly want to live in harmony with the world around us, it's time to expand our circle of compassion to include every living creature.

When questioned about the morality of eating animals, people often justify their actions through various excuses be it the food chain, personal choice, or the livelihood of butchers. However, at the core of it, the only undeniable reason remains **taste**. Most admit that eating meat satisfies their *desire*, not *need*. It's a matter of prioritizing momentary pleasure over a life's existence. The brutal truth is often ignored for the convenience of ignorance. As one interviewee candidly stated, ***"I like the taste. It is wrong morally, but I am prioritizing my desires."*** This admission uncovers the conflict within: while people recognize the ethical dilemma, they choose to suppress their conscience because facing the reality demands change. Just as Mahatma Gandhi once stood for the oppressed, perhaps one day humanity will stand for the voiceless acknowledging that every creature, even a chicken, has a fundamental right to live. After all, awareness is the first step toward change, and someone needs to advocate for those who cannot speak for themselves.

Why Advertisements Promote Eggs and Milk Over Vegetables Like Onions and Tomatoes

The frequent advertisements for products like eggs and milk, rather than vegetables like onions and tomatoes, reflect a strategic approach by industries to market goods that are not necessarily basic necessities but rather items they aim to promote for higher consumption and sales.

Eggs and milk are often branded as essential for health, with messaging centered around their nutritional benefits protein, calcium, and vitamins. These products are heavily industrialized and supported by large-scale farming industries with substantial budgets for marketing campaigns. Their promotion is also backed by historical narratives emphasizing their importance in a balanced diet, particularly in Western culture, where dairy and eggs have been staples of nutrition campaigns.

On the other hand, vegetables like onions and tomatoes are considered everyday essentials in most households and do not require extensive advertising. Their demand is consistent and driven by necessity, rather than persuasion. These vegetables are also primarily produced by small-scale farmers or local markets, which often lack the financial resources to fund large marketing campaigns.

The goal of advertising eggs, milk, and similar products is to create a perception of added value. The industries focus on building consumer demand by associating these items with health benefits, convenience, or even lifestyle choices. For example, milk advertisements often target parents by promoting its role in children's growth, while egg campaigns highlight their versatility and protein content.

Additionally, eggs and milk are products with a shorter shelf life, making consistent sales crucial for profitability. Advertising ensures a steady demand, reducing the risk of surplus or waste. In contrast, vegetables like onions and tomatoes naturally enjoy consistent demand as they are indispensable in daily cooking, requiring little to no promotional push.

Humans: The Only Species That Consumes Another Animal's Milk

Have you ever observed an animal drinking the milk of another species? For example, have you seen a donkey drinking the milk of a monkey? The answer is likely no. In the natural world, animals instinctively consume only the milk of their own species, and that too only during infancy, when milk is biologically necessary for their growth and development.

Humans, however, are unique in this regard. We are the only species that continues to consume milk beyond infancy, and not just our own primarily, we drink the milk of other animals, such as cows, goats, and buffaloes. This practice, which began thousands of years ago with the advent of animal domestication, has become a cultural norm in many parts of the world.

While milk is promoted as a rich source of nutrients like calcium and protein, it is worth reflecting on this distinctive human habit. Unlike other animals, whose dietary needs naturally evolve as they grow, humans have developed agricultural systems and societal norms that encourage the consumption of milk from other species throughout life. This raises interesting questions about our dietary choices and their alignment with natural biological needs.

Perhaps it is time to reevaluate the role of milk in our diets and consider whether our dependence on another species' milk is as essential as we have been led to believe.

The only nutrient missing in a vegan diet is Vitamin B12, which comes from bacteria found in animal products. However, B12 supplements are incredibly affordable, costing as little for weeks of use, making them accessible even for those on a tight budget.

Imagine, for a moment, being reborn as a chicken, a pig, a cow, or any other animal commonly consumed as food. But here's the twist your memories from your previous life as a human remain intact. You remember everything: the meals you enjoyed, the animals you consumed without hesitation, and the choices you made with little thought to the lives affected. Now, in this new form, you're no longer at the top of the food chain. Instead, you're the one trapped, awaiting an inevitable fate.

Picture the sheer helplessness you'd feel. You'd know exactly what's coming being confined in a cage, deprived of freedom, and eventually slaughtered. You'd cry out, but no one would care. To them, you're just a commodity, a meal on their plate, your life stripped down to a product of convenience. The irony would be inescapable: once, you were the one making choices that perpetuated this cycle, and now you're the victim of the very system you once supported.

Imagine watching someone sharpen their tools, preparing to turn you into their next meal. The fear would be unbearable. Would you beg for mercy? Would you feel betrayed by the humanity you once championed? How bitter would the realization be that in your previous life, you had the power to choose compassion, yet you chose convenience instead?

This exercise in empathy isn't meant to inspire guilt but rather awareness. Animals, just like humans, experience pain, fear, and the innate desire to live. They cry out in their final moments, just as we would if the roles were reversed. The only difference between them and us is the form we were born into a difference that has been used to justify unspeakable cruelty.

If you found yourself in their position, wouldn't you hope for compassion? Wouldn't you pray for someone to speak up, to break the cycle of violence? We often pride ourselves on our humanity, on our capacity for reason, empathy, and moral choices. But how often do we extend these qualities to the most vulnerable beings in our care?

Next time you sit down for a meal, pause and reflect: What if the tables were turned? What if it were you in that cage, destined to become someone else's food? And most importantly, what kind of world do you want to create a world that perpetuates suffering or one that embraces compassion and respect for all living beings?

This thought experiment is not just about imagining fear; it's about awakening responsibility. It's about recognizing that our choices today ripple far beyond our own lives. It's about realizing that every bite we take, every decision we make, has the power to either perpetuate harm or pave the way for a kinder, more compassionate world.

Some non-vegetarians often argue that vegetarians also consume living beings, such as fruits, grains, and vegetables, which come from living plants. They claim this makes vegetarians no different from non-vegetarians in terms of consuming life. However, this argument oversimplifies the reality and misses a crucial distinction.

Vegetarians consume a plant-based diet directly, relying on fruits, vegetables, grains, and other plant-based foods. These plants, while alive, do not possess a central nervous system, consciousness, or the ability to feel pain and fear like animals do. On the other hand, non-vegetarians consume animals such as cows, pigs, chickens, and others, which are sentient beings capable of experiencing suffering.

If consider you stuck on island surrounded by water presents a survival scenario where the primary instinct is to stay alive. In such extreme circumstances, morality often takes a back seat to necessity. If the only way to survive is to kill a creature for food, the decision becomes one of survival versus starvation. It's not about desire or preference but about doing what is essential to sustain life. While it would be heartbreaking to take a life, the harsh reality of survival pushes individuals to make choices they might never consider under normal circumstances. However, even in such situations, the act would not be taken lightly. There would be a sense of respect for the life being taken, acknowledging the sacrifice made for survival. This situation underscores the complexity of human morality how it can shift in life-or-death scenarios and the profound connection between survival and the ethical dilemmas we face when survival comes at the cost of another life.

The debate between vegetarianism and non-vegetarianism boils down to a fundamental question: ***What kind of relationship do we want to have with the world around us?*** If every life matters, then how do we justify taking the life of a sentient being for something as fleeting as a meal? It's not about vilifying those who eat meat but about encouraging reflection. When we have the ability to choose compassion, why not make that choice? After all, the act of killing an animal isn't just about physical sustenance it's a profound moral decision. And in that moment, we must ask ourselves:

• • •

Who gave us the right to play God?

• • •

CHAPTER IX

Good Things and Bad Things

Good things and bad things are inseparable elements of the human experience, each playing a crucial role in shaping our lives and perspectives. Good things often bring moments of joy, peace, and contentment, from the warmth of a comforting hug to the excitement of personal achievements. These moments, big or small, serve as reminders of what is valuable in life, reinforcing a sense of purpose, connection, and happiness. Whether it's the simple pleasure of a delicious meal, the beauty of a sunset, or the love of family and friends, good things often feel like gifts that restore our spirits and give us the energy to face the challenges ahead.

In Hindu scriptures, the distinction between good and bad is deeply rooted in the concepts of *Dharma* (righteousness), *Adharma* (unrighteousness), and the balance between virtue and vice. An example from Hindu teachings can be found in the ancient epic, the *Mahabharata*, particularly in the story of King Yudhishthira, the eldest of the Pandavas.

During the *Kurukshetra War*, a great battle between the Pandavas and the Kauravas, Yudhishthira was faced with difficult choices that tested his moral compass. In one instance, he was forced to make decisions that appeared to go against his personal desires or the conventional idea of what was "good." However, the scriptures teach that true good often requires one to prioritize the greater good over personal gain.

For example, during the *Game of Dice* (where the Pandavas lost everything), Yudhishthira was urged by his mother, Kunti, and his elders to uphold his responsibility as a leader, despite the suffering it caused him. His decision to accept his fate and go into exile, despite the loss of his kingdom, was seen as an act of selflessness and adherence to *Dharma*, even though it seemed like a "bad" situation at the time. This highlights a key aspect of Hindu philosophy: sometimes, what appears to be bad such as personal suffering or sacrifice is actually a path toward a greater moral purpose, and eventually leads to the victory of truth and righteousness.

Conversely, the actions of Duryodhana, the leader of the Kauravas, illustrate the concept of *Adharma*. His refusal to abide by the rules of *Dharma* and his constant manipulation of situations for his personal gain, despite the harm it caused others, was considered "bad" in the scriptures. Duryodhana's actions led to conflict, destruction, and his eventual downfall, symbolizing the inevitable defeat of unrighteousness.

The story teaches that good and bad are not always black and white. A righteous act may seem difficult or even "bad" in the short term, but ultimately, it leads to moral victory and spiritual growth. On the other hand, actions born of selfishness, greed, and disregard for Dharma, no matter how they may seem to offer short-term rewards, inevitably lead to harm and destruction. Hindu scriptures emphasize that good is not always easy, and bad is not always obvious it is the deeper understanding of *Dharma* that helps distinguish between the two.

However, bad things are just as much a part of the equation, often showing up as struggles, losses, or setbacks. These events may initially feel like obstacles, and at times, they can weigh heavily on our hearts. Loss, failure, pain, and disappointment often shake our sense of security and make us question the fairness of life. But in reality, bad things have the potential to serve as powerful teachers. They force us to confront our vulnerabilities, weaknesses, and fears, often leading to deeper self-reflection. Through overcoming adversity, we discover new strengths, develop resilience, and gain a greater appreciation for the good things when they come.

In real life, the distinction between good and bad often exists in a grey area, where the lines blur depending on one's perspective, values, and the context of the situation. Consider the act of a person helping an elderly neighbor with groceries. On the surface, this seems like an unquestionable "good" act. The act is rooted in kindness, empathy, and a sense of community. Not only does it make the neighbor's day a little easier, but it also brings joy to the helper, reinforcing the bonds of human connection. This small but meaningful gesture is a reflection of the human capacity for compassion and care. It exemplifies how something as simple as helping a neighbor can ripple out into a larger effect, creating an environment of mutual support and trust.

But life is far from simple, and sometimes, acts we might consider "good" carry unintended consequences. Take, for example, the case of a person who donates a large sum of money to a charity. On the surface, it's a noble gesture helping those in need and giving back to the community. However, when you dig deeper, you may find that the charity doesn't use the donations wisely, or perhaps the donation is made for selfish reasons, such as gaining social recognition or tax benefits. In such a scenario, the intention behind the action shifts the nature of the act itself. What seemed like a good deed becomes complex when examined from a different lens.

Then there's the contrast of actions deemed "bad" or harmful. Imagine someone spreading false rumors about a friend, intentionally damaging their reputation. At first glance, this may seem like a "bad" action self-serving, harmful, and malicious. Yet, even in this seemingly negative act, there may be hidden layers. The person spreading the rumors might feel insecure or threatened, projecting their fears onto others. From this angle, their actions stem from an inner turmoil or a need for validation, rather than pure malice. Recognizing these underlying causes doesn't excuse the harm done but brings awareness to the complexities of human behavior.

In another scenario, think of a doctor who faces the challenging decision of whether to administer a painful treatment to save a patient's life. The decision seems cruel at first, as it forces the patient to endure temporary suffering. Yet, in the broader context, this action is a form of "good." The doctor's intent is to preserve life, even if the process is uncomfortable in the short term. This story reflects the idea that sometimes, doing what is necessary and right may not always feel pleasant. It highlights the paradox of "good" and "bad" being intertwined and evolving based on time, intent, and consequences.

There are also moments in life when an action's morality isn't clear until the passage of time allows for reflection. For instance, parents who impose strict discipline on their children may seem harsh at the moment, but years later, their children may come to realize that those lessons shaped them into responsible and respectful adults. This creates the age-old question: Was it "bad" in the moment for the child, or was it part of a greater, long-term "good"?

Real-life examples like these show that the journey from what is perceived as good or bad is not always a straightforward path. It's not just about the action itself but the intent behind it, the ripple effects it causes, and the long-term impact it leaves on people and communities. Understanding that "good" and "bad" are fluid terms allows us to approach life with more empathy, awareness, and a deeper understanding of the human experience. Each person's story is layered with complexities, and each decision, no matter how seemingly small, can have ripples that affect countless others in ways we might never fully understand.

Moreover, the contrast between good and bad things enhances our ability to find balance and meaning. If life were entirely without struggle, we might take the good things for granted or not fully appreciate their significance. It is through hardship that we learn to savor the light moments and understand the depth of joy and fulfillment. The combination of both good and bad things allows us to develop empathy, patience, and wisdom. It is this balance that ultimately helps us navigate life with a sense of gratitude and understanding, knowing that both joy and sorrow are essential to living a rich, meaningful life.

The concept of good and bad is a deeply personal and fluid one, often shaped by individual perspectives, societal values, and the situations we find ourselves in. What we consider good or bad can vary dramatically depending on the context, experiences, and the ever-changing circumstances of life. For instance, imagine a person who, after years of struggling in an unfulfilling job, decides to quit and pursue their passion. In the moment, the decision may seem daunting, even "bad," because it comes with uncertainty, fear of failure, and financial strain. But as time goes by, they discover a sense of purpose and fulfillment they never imagined. The same decision that once seemed bad ultimately leads them to a life they are proud of a life they never would have experienced had they not taken the risk.

On the other hand, what seems "good" at first glance may, over time, reveal itself to be harmful. Consider someone who decides to take a shortcut in their work, thinking it will help them achieve success more quickly. Initially, the result may be rewarding a promotion, an accolade, or recognition. But as they continue down this path, they realize that their shortcut has compromised their integrity, strained relationships with colleagues, and diminished their sense of self-worth. The initial "good" feeling was merely a façade, and what seemed like a shortcut to success turned into a long-term lesson in the importance of honesty and hard work.

Life is full of moments where what we perceive as good or bad shifts as we move through different experiences. Take, for example, a person who suffers a devastating personal loss. In the wake of their grief, the world may seem bleak, and everything about their circumstances may feel overwhelmingly bad. Yet, over time, they begin to learn new lessons about themselves, their strength, and their resilience. What once felt like the end of the road becomes the beginning of a new chapter a more enlightened, compassionate version of themselves.

The story of good and bad is not one of fixed definitions but rather one of evolution. Our judgments are shaped by the challenges we face, the decisions we make, and the wisdom we gain along the way. It's the ongoing narrative of learning from our mistakes, reevaluating our choices, and growing from our experiences. Every decision, whether it leads to success or failure, offers an opportunity for reflection, growth, and a deeper understanding of life's complexities. Sometimes, what we consider bad today may turn out to be the very thing we needed to experience to reach a better tomorrow.

Where does the journey of "Good" and "Bad" truly end? The answer lies in **Mukti** freedom from the endless cycle of birth, death, and rebirth. Mukti, or liberation, is not about choosing between good and bad, nor is it about avoiding karma altogether. It is about transcending the very idea of duality. Good and bad are like chains one made of gold and the other of iron. Both may appear different, but they bind us just the same. To achieve Mukti, one must break free from these chains.

But how does a human being attain Mukti while still alive, bound by karma and its consequences? Every action we perform, whether good or bad, creates an imprint a karmic seed that perpetuates our cycle of existence. The secret to liberation lies not in the action itself but in how we approach it.

The key is **detachment**. A person achieves freedom by performing their duties without being attached to the results. This principle, often referred to as **Nishkama Karma**, teaches us to act with full sincerity and effort, yet remain indifferent to the outcome. When you work without the expectation of reward or fear of failure, your karma ceases to bind you. The attachment to results whether it's pride in success or despair in failure is what creates the chains that tether us to this cycle. Let go of these attachments, and you begin to taste the essence of Mukti.

This state of freedom doesn't mean abandoning life or responsibility. It means living fully, performing every action with a pure heart, and accepting whatever outcome comes as part of the larger cosmic order. It's about surrendering the ego that constantly seeks validation through success or broods over failure. True freedom comes when the mind is no longer enslaved by desires, fears, and judgments.

To achieve Mukti, one must also cultivate mindfulness and self-awareness. By observing the mind and its tendencies, you can transcend the impulses that keep you trapped in cycles of craving and aversion. Meditation, introspection, and selfless service are tools that help purify the mind, allowing you to rise above the polarities of good and bad.

In the end, Mukti is not an escape from life; it is the ultimate freedom within life. It is realizing that you are not the doer but merely an instrument of the divine will. It is the understanding that good and bad, success and failure, joy and sorrow are all transient. When you embrace this truth, the chains fall away, and you experience the boundless peace of liberation.

Mukti is the state where the soul is no longer weighed down by the baggage of karma. It is freedom not just from the physical world but from the illusions of the mind. And this freedom is attainable not by running away from life but by engaging with it fully, without attachment, with a heart free of desires and a mind free of judgment.

CHAPTER X

Which Is Better for You: Cold or Hot?

When it comes to deciding whether cold or hot is better for you, the answer isn't always straightforward, as it often depends on the situation, your body's needs, and personal preferences. Cold and hot both have distinct benefits that serve different purposes. Cold temperatures can be refreshing, especially during a scorching summer day. Imagine stepping outside into the heat, feeling the weight of the sun's rays pressing down on you. A cold drink, a splash of water, or even a cool breeze can immediately lift your spirits and help your body avoid overheating. Cold therapy, like an ice pack on a sprained ankle, works wonders in reducing inflammation, numbing pain, and speeding up the healing process. I remember the first time I twisted my ankle during a soccer match. I quickly grabbed ice from the cooler, and as the coldness numbed the pain, I realized how effectively it worked to reduce the swelling. Cold constricts the blood vessels, limiting blood flow to the affected area, which prevents further damage and helps in quicker recovery.

On the other hand, hot temperatures bring comfort, warmth, and relaxation. Think of a chilly winter night, when you're wrapped in a cozy blanket with a hot cup of tea in hand, and the warmth slowly spreads through your body, melting away the cold. Hot water soothes sore muscles and stiff joints. It was on a cold evening, after a long and exhausting day, when I slipped into a hot bath, letting the steam rise around me, and I could feel my body unwind and relax in a way that cold temperatures could never offer. Heat increases blood circulation, helping to relieve tension and improve flexibility. It has the power to calm the mind and bring a sense of peace, as your muscles and nerves loosen up from the warmth.

But choosing between cold and hot isn't always clear-cut it depends on what your body is telling you in the moment. After an intense workout, cold may be your go-to for reducing inflammation and preventing soreness. However, when you want to unwind after a long day, heat may offer the relief and comfort your mind and body need. In certain cases, alternating between hot and cold can bring balance, as both stimulate the body in unique ways. Ultimately, whether it's cold or hot, the choice is personal, shaped by individual experience, context, and the body's immediate needs. Each has its place in supporting health and wellness, and the key is to listen to your body, knowing when to embrace the chill and when to enjoy the warmth.

It was a dark, eerie night in the survival game of life. The sky above was as black as ink, and the ground beneath my feet seemed to pulse with uncertainty. The host, a mysterious figure cloaked in shadows, stood before me, an enigmatic grin on their face. With a gesture of their hand, a glowing screen appeared, and the words flickered: "Choose your path: 50-degree heat or -50-degree cold."

I stood there, heart racing. The heat of 50 degrees unbearable, almost suffocating, like walking into the belly of a fiery beast, the air thick and heavy, pressing against my lungs. I could imagine the sweat pouring down, my body dehydrating under the relentless sun. It would be a test of endurance, pushing my physical limits to the edge, fighting every step to keep moving. Could I survive that? How long could I bear the searing heat before my strength waned, before the heat consumed me entirely?

Then, I thought about the cold, a biting -50 degrees. I could already feel the frost creeping up my spine just at the thought of it. It was like being trapped in an endless winter, with no escape, no warmth. My breath would freeze in front of me, my fingers and toes becoming stiff and numb. It would be a battle against the elements, a fight for survival against the very chill that threatened to freeze my blood. Would I even have the mental fortitude to endure such cold for long? My body would start shutting down, each step becoming harder as the cold crept deeper into my bones.

As I stood there, the decision weighing heavily on me, I remembered a moment from my past, a small but pivotal memory that helped me make my choice. A summer day long ago, when I'd walked across a desert, feeling the unbearable heat scorch my skin. I had collapsed, exhausted, my water long gone. Just when I thought I couldn't go on, I found an oasis, a patch of cool shade and a sip of water. The relief was overwhelming. It had been the heat that had taught me about my limits and resilience, and how finding refuge when everything seemed unbearable made survival possible. But in the end, it was the cold I feared more.

With a deep breath, I chose the heat. I knew that in extreme heat, I had a fighting chance finding shelter, taking breaks, and drinking water could help me survive. The cold, however, had a way of slowly stealing away your strength without mercy. It was silent, patient, and far more insidious than the heat. It would take away your will before you even knew it.

The host nodded, almost as if they knew the choice I would make. A door materialized in front of me, a gateway to the unknown. I stepped through, ready to face whatever challenges awaited me in the scorching heat. I knew it wouldn't be easy, but I was determined to survive, to push through the suffocating air and the blinding sun. As I walked into the unknown, I reminded myself that life is about endurance, about facing the elements and choosing to fight, no matter how overwhelming the circumstances may seem.

In that moment, I realized that survival isn't about what's easier it's about understanding your limits, accepting the harshness of life, and finding a way to endure. The heat might have been unbearable, but it was a challenge I could face, step by painful step.

• • •

Conclusion: In general, the human body can only withstand high temperatures for short periods, and it's vital to stay hydrated, avoid prolonged exposure to extreme heat, and seek shelter or cooling methods when necessary. The probability of survival in both extreme conditions is heavily dependent on available resources. In extreme heat, you could survive longer if you have water and shade, but without these resources, heat can be a relentless killer. In extreme cold, survival chances drop faster without shelter and warmth, but with the right tools, it is possible to survive. In both cases, the ability to secure the right resources (water, shelter, food) is crucial, and the survival probability in both situations would be a narrow window, requiring careful planning, resilience, and resourcefulness.

• • •

CHAPTER XI

Nature's Gift

• • •

"The most environmentally friendly product is the one you didn't buy"
| Joshua Becker, American author

• • •

As the title, **Nature's Gift**, this topic is dedicated to understanding and preserving the treasures that nature offers us. At the very beginning, I've included a quote: **"The most environmentally friendly product is the one you didn't buy."** You might wonder how this applies here, given that purchasing this book required paper, ink, and other resources for its printing. How, then, can this book be considered environmentally friendly?

The answer lies in understanding the essence of being environmentally conscious. It does not mean avoiding everything or refusing to use any resources in our daily lives. Rather, it is about identifying our true necessities and making mindful choices accordingly. While writing this book, I, too, questioned whether it was the right decision to use these resources. However, I realized that if this book helps you embrace a more sustainable way of living, then it fulfills its purpose. My goal is simple: if reading this book inspires you to think critically about your choices what to buy and what not to buy then every page and drop of ink used to create it is justified.

As you reading this book, you take each breath effortlessly, filling your lungs with air rich in oxygen a life-sustaining gift you rarely pause to consider. Have you ever wondered where this oxygen comes from? It's the silent labor of trees, plants, and tiny oceanic phytoplankton that work tirelessly, turning sunlight into this invisible elixir of life through the miraculous process of photosynthesis. This oxygen doesn't just sustain you it connects every living being on this planet, forming an unbroken thread that ties us all to nature. Without it, life as we know it wouldn't exist.

And as your fingers brush against the pages of this book, have you reflected on their origin? These pages once belonged to majestic trees that stood tall, their branches reaching for the skies, their roots digging deep into the Earth. They provided shade, shelter, and sustenance to countless creatures, playing their role in the intricate web of life. Now, they've taken on a new purpose to share stories, knowledge, and wisdom, connecting human thought across time and space.

Both the air you breathe and the pages you hold are testaments to nature's generosity. They are gifts freely given, requiring nothing in return but a sense of respect and stewardship. With every breath, every touch of paper, you are reminded of the beauty and interconnectedness of the natural world. It's a silent symphony, a continuous cycle of giving and receiving, where nature sustains and nurtures us in ways we often take for granted.

You might be sitting on a chair, resting comfortably, or perhaps lying on a bed, relaxed and at ease. Have you ever wondered where these everyday objects came from? The wood in your chair or bed was once part of a tree a living, breathing organism that stood tall in a forest, providing shade, oxygen, and a home to countless creatures. Its roots stretched deep into the earth, drawing strength from the soil, while its branches reached for the skies, embracing the sun and wind. Even the metal or fabric that supports your weight has its origins in nature. The metal was mined from deep within the Earth, where it lay hidden for millennia, and the fabric might be woven from cotton, which grew in fields, nurtured by sunlight and rain. Everything you use, everything that makes your life comfortable, is a gift from nature a quiet testament to the Earth's boundless generosity. These gifts remind us of our deep connection to the natural world, urging us to cherish and protect the very source of our comfort and existence.

As you turn each page, think about the countless hands of nature that have made this moment possible from the winds that carried seeds to fertile soil to the sunlight and rain that nourished the forests, to the unseen ecosystems that quietly work to maintain the delicate balance of life. Every word you read is an opportunity to reflect on the remarkable gift of existence, a gift that we owe entirely to the Earth and its timeless wisdom.

Nature's gift to us is an abundant and awe-inspiring treasure, offering a wealth of resources that sustain life in all its forms. From the very air we breathe to the water that nourishes our bodies, nature is the foundation of our existence. It provides us with food, shelter, and raw materials that fuel our industries, from timber for construction to minerals for technology. The soil beneath our feet is rich with the nutrients that enable plants to grow, sustaining both wildlife and human civilizations for millennia. Beyond physical sustenance, nature offers intangible gifts that enrich our lives beauty, serenity, and inspiration. The vibrant colors of blooming flowers, the sound of birdsong at dawn, the rustling of leaves in a gentle breeze, and the infinite stars in the night sky all speak to the wonder of the natural world. These experiences connect us to something greater than ourselves, reminding us of the fragile and interconnected web of life.

Nature's gifts also include the healing power of its plants, animals, and landscapes. For centuries, humans have relied on natural remedies herbs, flowers, and trees to cure ailments, ease stress, and improve well-being. The therapeutic effects of nature are not only physical but also psychological. Time spent in natural surroundings has been shown to reduce anxiety, increase creativity, and promote overall mental health. A walk through the forest or a moment of quiet reflection by the ocean can restore our sense of balance and peace in ways that material possessions cannot.

The magnificence of nature also lies in its diversity. Each ecosystem, from the deepest oceans to the highest mountain peaks, supports unique species and forms of life, many of which have yet to be discovered. This biological richness is a gift in itself, as it provides opportunities for learning, discovery, and scientific advancement. The study of nature has led to groundbreaking innovations in medicine, agriculture, and technology, all of which have improved the quality of life for people around the world.

To achieve what you truly desire in life, you must often do the opposite of what seems logical. If you wish to become strong, first embrace lightness and humility. If you seek wealth, learn to give generously and spend with purpose. If you aspire to be powerful, begin by staying hidden and working quietly in the shadows. If you desire wisdom, embrace the mindset of knowing nothing, for only an open mind can absorb true knowledge. This is the law of nature the paradoxical truth that opposites fuel balance and growth.

Only something cold can generate heat within itself. Only what is dry can soak up the essence of moisture. Whatever begins must eventually end, and whatever ends gives birth to something new. The entire universe thrives on the harmony of opposites a delicate interplay known as *Yin and Yang* in Chinese philosophy or *Taoism*, the path of balance. The light exists because of the dark; life has meaning because of death. This duality defines existence, creating the eternal dance of opposites that shape our reality.

To find true fulfillment, you must align yourself with this balance. Do not force the natural flow of life or resist its rhythm. When you try too hard to control everything, you upset the balance and lose the essence of the journey. Instead, embrace *The Tao* the way of being. Be present, live authentically, and remove the weight of expectation from your actions. Let go of the desire for immediate results, for the universe rewards those who work patiently in harmony with its cycles.

True strength lies in adaptability, not resistance. True wisdom lies in simplicity, not complexity. When you remove the pressure of outcomes from your efforts, you free yourself to act with clarity and purpose. The universe thrives on balance, and by aligning with its laws, you allow success, happiness, and fulfillment to flow naturally into your life.

Accept the paradox of life. Live light to become strong. Give to grow richer. Stay hidden to rise above. Know nothing to understand everything. This is the path of nature's harmony a life lived not by forcing, but by being, and trusting in the balance of all things.

Have you ever wondered why nature provides us with such abundant resources? From the air we breathe to the food we consume; nature seems to offer everything we need to survive and thrive. But what does nature ask in return? The answer lies in reproduction the continuation of life through each new generation. Nature's true purpose in granting us these resources is not merely for our own enjoyment or survival, but for the perpetuation of life itself. By bringing new life into the world, we fulfill nature's fundamental cycle, ensuring that the chain of life continues. Through reproduction, we not only contribute to the survival of our species but also to the balance and vitality of the entire ecosystem. It is through the legacy of each new generation that we honor the gifts of nature, perpetuating its cycles and maintaining the harmony of the natural world.

However, with these gifts comes great responsibility. As stewards of the Earth, we have a duty to protect and preserve the environment for future generations. Human activities, such as deforestation, pollution, and overconsumption, threaten the delicate balance of ecosystems that provide us with these gifts. Climate change is a stark reminder that our actions have far-reaching consequences, not only for ourselves but for the entire planet. In recognizing the value of nature's gifts, we must act with intention and care to ensure that these resources are available for those who will come after us. Conservation efforts, sustainable practices, and respect for the Earth are essential in safeguarding nature's gifts.

Ultimately, nature's gift is a reminder of our interconnectedness with the world around us. It calls us to live in harmony with the environment, to cherish the beauty and abundance it offers, and to be mindful of the impact we have on the planet. By nurturing our relationship with nature, we can ensure that its gifts continue to sustain life and inspire wonder for generations to come.

CHAPTER XII

I'm Lucky

Have you ever wondered why I say you are lucky? Let me explain. Imagine an ideal person someone with two eyes to see, two hands to work, two legs to move, and all five senses functioning perfectly. If you possess these abilities, you are already incredibly fortunate. Think about it millions of people face challenges every day, whether it's due to disabilities, illnesses, or circumstances beyond their control. The fact that you have a body that allows you to navigate life, to see the beauty around you, to hear the sounds of the world, and to feel and experience life in its fullness is nothing short of a blessing.

And there's more to it. If you are reading this book, it means your mind is actively processing these words, understanding their meaning, and engaging with the ideas. That, too, is a sign of incredible luck. Your brain a marvel of nature allows you to think, learn, and grow. It empowers you to dream, to create, and to connect with the world in profound ways. This ability to read and comprehend is not something to take for granted. Millions around the globe lack access to education or suffer from cognitive impairments that make such experiences inaccessible.

So, take a moment to recognize how lucky you truly are. You have a body that works, a mind that thinks, and the opportunity to expand your knowledge and grow as a person. These gifts are not universal they are precious privileges. Life's daily challenges often make us forget the simple things we should be grateful for, but when we pause to reflect, we realize how much we already have. Embrace this luck, cherish it, and use it wisely.

"I am lucky" is not just a phrase, but a mindset, a declaration of appreciation for the good things in life, however big or small. It signifies the recognition that, despite the inevitable struggles, setbacks, and hardships that everyone faces, there are countless elements of fortune, serendipity, and privilege that contribute to our overall well-being. Being able to say "I am lucky" is a reflection of gratitude for the positive aspects of life, from the everyday comforts to the extraordinary moments. It's the awareness that not everyone has the same opportunities or experiences, and for that reason, we should never take for granted what we have.

Sometimes, luck is visible in the simplest of things: waking up to a beautiful morning, receiving an unexpected compliment, or finding moments of peace amid the chaos. It can come in the form of people who care about us, a sudden opportunity that changes the course of our day, or a small act of kindness that brightens our outlook. Feeling lucky can also mean acknowledging the privilege of good health, financial stability, a roof over our heads, or the support systems we have in place. These are the things that many people may lack, but for those who have them, they are invaluable sources of good fortune.

Luck can also be found in our ability to navigate challenges with resilience, to learn from failures, and to grow stronger from difficult experiences. It is the perspective that, even in moments of adversity, there are lessons to be learned and wisdom to be gained. Being able to look back on life with a sense of gratitude, rather than regret, is one of the greatest forms of luck that one can have.

In many ways, "I am lucky" is a mindset that enables us to focus on what we have, rather than what we lack. It encourages us to embrace the present moment and appreciate the blessings that surround us, from the relationships we cherish to the opportunities we may take for granted. By acknowledging our good fortune, we develop a greater sense of contentment, humility, and empathy for those who may not share the same privileges.

Moreover, luck is not only about chance or random occurrences. It is also about the actions we take to create opportunities for ourselves. Sometimes, luck is the result of hard work, perseverance, and staying open to new possibilities. When we maintain an optimistic attitude, take chances, and remain hopeful in the face of uncertainty, we often find that luck is more likely to come our way.

It is as though our attitude towards life invites positive energy and new possibilities into our lives.

To say "I am lucky" is to acknowledge both the external circumstances that have helped shape our lives and the internal mindset that allows us to thrive. It's a reminder that, despite life's imperfections, there is always something to be grateful for. Whether it's the love of family and friends, the ability to learn and grow, or the opportunities that come unexpectedly, luck is a combination of both fortune and perspective. When we truly recognize how lucky we are, we are inspired to give back, to share our good fortune with others, and to contribute to making the world a better place.

I choose to embrace the power of luck in my life. I consciously decide to be a lucky person and attract all the good things that the universe has to offer. Every day, I affirm that I am incredibly lucky. Those around me are often amazed by how fortunate I am, and I continually experience the flow of good fortune. I feel lucky, and I know that everything always works out for me, no matter the circumstances. I am filled with good luck, and I attract positive energy and opportunities wherever I go.

Good luck is not only something I encounter; it is my natural vibration. I allow myself to feel lucky all the time, and I expect wonderful things to happen to me. I simply ask for what I want and allow the universe to deliver, knowing that good things are always coming my way. My life is overflowing with opportunities, and I trust that I am in the right place at the right time. I am a winner in every aspect of life, and my good luck continues to grow.

I attract good fortune with ease, and my positive mindset helps me manifest the best possibilities. Whether at work, in my personal life, or in my interactions with others, good luck finds me wherever I go. I am a magnet for prosperity and happiness, and every day brings new reasons to be grateful for my good fortune. I am aligned with the blessings of the universe, and good luck flows into my life effortlessly.

I love the feeling of being lucky, and I trust that Lady Luck smiles down on me at all times. I carry an aura of good luck with me, and those around me benefit from it as well. My good fortune spreads to others, creating an environment filled with abundance and joy. I am deeply grateful for my luck, and I express gratitude for the blessings that come my way.

Good luck is not just a fleeting moment; it is a constant presence in my life. I am a good luck magnet, and I draw success, happiness, and prosperity with every step I take. My life is a testament to the power of positivity, and I know that my luck is limitless. Today, and every day, I choose to embrace my luck and allow it to guide me toward even greater success and fulfillment.

As I continue on my journey, I recognize that luck is a part of who I am. I am lucky by nature, and I will always be blessed with good fortune. No matter where I go or what I do, I attract good luck, and I am eternally grateful for the gifts the universe bestows upon me. I am truly one of the luckiest people alive, and I let that luck guide me toward a life full of love, prosperity, and success.

I am truly blessed with an abundance of good luck and Fortune that flows into my life effortlessly every day. I am constantly vibrating with the frequency of good luck, and I trust that the universe is always guiding me toward the best opportunities. Good luck follows me wherever I go, and I am a magnet for Fortune. Everything in my life is always working out for my highest good, and I am grateful for the positive energy that surrounds me. I know that my good luck is ever-present, and it is a natural part of who I am.

I have a deep belief that every day holds new blessings for me. I attract good luck with ease, and I am aligned with the positive vibrations of the universe. Every moment, I am in tune with the energy of success, and I expect only the best to happen for me. I am confident that everything I desire is already on its way to me. The law of attraction works in my favor, bringing me the best outcomes and guiding me to the right places at the right times.

I am a good luck charm not just for myself, but also for others. I bring positive energy wherever I go, and my life is filled with opportunities, prosperity, and blessings. My life is a reflection of the universe's support, and I am grateful for the abundance that surrounds me. Each day is a new opportunity for me to embrace the good luck and blessings that are already here. I trust that everything is working out for me, even when things seem uncertain.

I trust in my intuition, and I believe that I am always in the right place at the right time. Everything I do aligns with my higher self, guiding me toward success and joy. I expect good things to happen, and I am always amazed by how effortlessly the universe provides for me. I believe in my worth, and I accept the goodness that flows into my life. The universe is constantly showing me signs of how everything is working out in my favor, and I am forever grateful for the flow of good fortune.

As I continue to move forward in life, I know that the universe is always conspiring in my favor. I am living a magical life, and my days are filled with joy, prosperity, and happiness. Every experience I encounter is a reflection of the good luck that surrounds me. I am a positive force in the world, and my energy uplifts those around me. I know that life is meant to be easy and that I am always supported by the universe. I am aligned with my purpose, and I trust that everything is unfolding for my highest good.

I am a lucky person, and my life is constantly improving. I expect the best, and the best always finds me. Good luck is my constant companion, and I know that every moment is a gift. My confidence grows each day as I continue to embrace the incredible blessings that life has to offer. The universe is always working with me to bring more abundance, and I welcome it with open arms.

I expect that everything in my life is always working out for me. Even when things don't seem to align perfectly, I trust that everything will fall into place in the end. I know that the universe is guiding me towards my highest good, and I am confident that my path is unfolding exactly as it should. I hold onto the belief that things are always working out for me, even if the situation doesn't look like it's going in my favor at first. I let go of worries and trust that all is happening for my benefit. The universe is conspiring in my favor, and I have faith that everything will align in perfect timing.

My motto is simple: everything is always working out for me. I have full confidence that whatever happens, I am exactly where I need to be, and the universe is always leading me toward the best possible outcomes. Whether it's something small like getting the best parking spot or bigger things like opportunities for personal and professional growth, I trust that the flow of good luck is constant in my life. I am a magnet for positivity, and good things keep coming my way.

Every day, I affirm that my life is full of wonderful opportunities, and I am open to receiving them. The more I focus on the good around me, the better comes into my life. I am filled with gratitude for the blessings I have and the ones that are yet to come. Every morning, I set my intention to be aware of the good in my life, and as I do, I discover more reasons to be thankful. I embrace the abundance of life, knowing that the universe is abundant and always providing.

I choose to focus on the positive, seeking out the good in every situation. When I look for reasons to smile, I always find them, and this positive energy expands into the world around me. My job is contagious, and I radiate positivity wherever I go. I attract friendly people, helpful situations, and opportunities that align with my dreams and desires. I am a beacon of light, spreading good vibes wherever I step.

My life just keeps getting better and better, and I allow joy and happiness to flood my being. Every step I take leads me to a brighter, more fulfilling future. I trust that my positive expectations are guiding me to experiences that uplift and support me. I wake up excited for each new day, knowing that it will bring more blessings and opportunities. I savor the small moments of beauty in my life, and I am constantly amazed at how everything keeps improving.

I am open to receiving all the good life has to offer. I know that when I focus on the good, better will come my way. This mindset transforms my life into a continuous flow of blessings. I intentionally choose joy and gratitude, knowing that this energy attracts even more positive experiences. I look for the good in the world, and the more I look, the better I see. I feel a deep sense of appreciation for the abundance in my life, and I welcome more of it each day.

With each passing moment, my life becomes richer with love, laughter, and good fortune. My positive intentions, gratitude, and clear vision are magnets for good things. I live a magical life, where every day brings new reasons to be grateful, and my life is full of amazing surprises. I trust that everything is always working out for me, and the more I believe in this truth, the more it becomes my reality. Today, and every day, I celebrate the good, knowing that the best is yet to come.

The essence of eliminating ego lies in freeing yourself from the chains of comparison. True liberation begins when you stop measuring yourself against others, for you are unique and incomparable in this vast universe. Your individuality is unparalleled there has never been, nor will there ever be, another like you.

Embracing this truth means accepting yourself entirely, as you are. It is not about striving to fit into someone else's mold but recognizing the inherent value in your existence. Your personality, your journey, and your essence are distinct, making you irreplaceable. To let go of ego is to find peace in this realization and to live authentically, without the weight of comparison or the need for validation.

Today, I choose to look for things around me that bring joy and positivity. Every person I meet will be greeted with a smile, and I will send love to everyone I come across. I will focus on seeing the goodness in the world, constantly searching for what is right and uplifting. The more I look for the good, the more I find, and in doing so, I spread this positivity to everyone and everything

I encounter. My good nature radiates and spreads, ensuring that everything around me is aligned with my highest good. I open my mind and heart to all the good things the world has to offer, embracing everything that brings joy, peace, and fulfillment into my life.

I celebrate all the goodness in my life, as wonderful things are constantly unfolding before me. My dreams and desires are manifesting in perfect harmony with the universe, and I can see them coming true right before my eyes. With each passing moment, my life gets better and better, filled with amazing opportunities and experiences. I am a magnet for abundance and all the gifts that the universe provides. I welcome these gifts with open arms and an open heart, as I know my life is truly blessed beyond my wildest imagination.

I am constantly surrounded by good fortune. Luck finds me at every turn, and I embrace it fully, knowing that the more I expect good things, the more they show up in my life. I am a walking good luck charm, and my good fortune extends to everyone around me. Today is my lucky day, and I know that luck is on my side, guiding me to success and happiness. I am winning at life, and everything I want and need comes to me effortlessly. The universe is always providing for me, ensuring that everything I desire is manifesting in perfect timing.

With each passing day, my life becomes more abundant, filled with opportunities, love, and success. I am open to receiving all the gifts that come my way, and I know that I am worthy of all the good things that the world has to offer. I am aligned with the energy of abundance, attracting more prosperity, love, and happiness into my life. As I continue to focus on the positive and expect the best, I create a reality where everything I desire comes to fruition. My dreams are becoming a beautiful reality, and I am truly living my best life, every single day.

Luck and good fortune follow me wherever I go, and I radiate positivity and abundance. I am constantly amazed by the miracles unfolding in my life. I am attracting more good things, and my life is becoming more magical with each passing day. My thoughts, actions, and beliefs are in perfect alignment with the abundance I desire, and I am a magnet for all the good things life has to offer. The universe is working in my favor, and I trust that everything is unfolding perfectly for me. Today, I embrace the limitless possibilities of the universe, knowing that I am deserving of all the blessings that come my way.

I am a magnet for good luck, and it constantly follows me wherever I go. Every day, my life is filled with blessings, and I attract fortune and positive experiences like a magnet. I choose to be a lucky person, and my good luck flows naturally into every aspect of my life. The universe seems to align with my desires, bringing me the best opportunities, and I am always in the right place at the right time. I feel incredibly lucky, and it's evident to everyone around me. Those who know me are constantly amazed by how effortlessly good things happen to me.

Good luck is not just a fleeting moment for me it is a part of my natural vibration. I am in tune with the energy of positivity, prosperity, and success. I believe that everything I do will lead to favorable outcomes, and my expectations are always filled with optimism. I am constantly surrounded by abundance and happiness, and I take time each day to appreciate the many blessings in my life. Life is not only magical; it is meant to be enjoyed. Every day is an opportunity for new and exciting things to unfold in my life.

I am a good luck charm, and my luck extends to those around me. As I continue to attract positive energy, I share it with everyone in my circle. My success, prosperity, and happiness have a ripple effect that touches the lives of others. The good fortune I experience encourages others to believe in their own potential and to recognize the abundance that surrounds them. I am a living example of how luck can be cultivated and shared, and as I continue to radiate positive energy, I draw better luck into my life.

Richard Wiseman conducted an experiment that divided people into two groups: those who considered themselves *lucky* and those who did not. The participants were asked to count the number of photos in a newspaper. Surprisingly, the people who considered themselves unlucky took an average of 2 minutes to count the photos, carefully scanning them one by one. However, those who saw themselves as lucky completed the task in just a few seconds. The reason? On the second page of the newspaper, there was a large headline that said, *"Stop counting! There are 43 photos in this newspaper."* Additionally, a note in the middle promised a reward of ₹250 if shown to the researcher. The so-called unlucky people missed this obvious sign, while the lucky ones noticed it and won the prize. This shows how perception plays a key role in identifying opportunities.

The difference between luck and chance lies in how we approach situations. Many believe that being lucky is about chance alone, but in reality, it's about the combination of *talent, hard work, and opportunity.* For example, in 2016, Leicester City's chances of winning the Premier League were seen as 5000 to 1 virtually impossible. Historically, the team had a poor track record. However, in 2016, their planning, practice, and performance were exceptional, leading them to a miraculous win. While people called it "luck," it was the team's hard work and strategic efforts that turned the odds in their favor.

Understanding situations carefully and making well-planned decisions can significantly increase your chances of success. For instance, consider a scenario where 90% of people fail at a certain task. Most would avoid it out of fear, focusing on the high failure rate. But if you study and analyze *why* 10% succeed, you might uncover valuable secrets and strategies to join that group. Often, success lies in thinking differently and taking calculated risks.

Statistical misconceptions also shape our beliefs. For example, studies show that 33% of Americans are overweight. This does not mean that anyone living in America has a 33% chance of being overweight. Your health, fitness, and habits depend on the choices *you make,* not on statistics alone. Similarly, people often misinterpret numbers without realizing that *how* we perceive and act upon these statistics makes all the difference.

A positive mindset is critical in overcoming challenges. Take the example of an athlete who faced ridicule for trying an unconventional high jump technique *the backward flip*. Initially, critics mocked him, but this unique approach helped him perform better than ever. He practiced diligently and eventually won an Olympic gold medal, silencing everyone who doubted him. This teaches us an important lesson: sometimes, breaking away from the crowd and trying something new can lead to incredible success.

Successful people often share a common trait: *passion* for their work and ***persistence*** in the face of failure. Jonathan Drop, a famous actor, is an example. Born in a small village with no exposure to the film industry, he moved to New York, worked as a waiter to pay for acting classes, and seized every opportunity. Though offered minor roles initially, Jonathan treated them as stepping stones, worked hard, and gradually built a successful career. His story reminds us that consistent effort and optimism can turn small chances into life-changing opportunities.

High expectations lead to better results a phenomenon proven by scientific experiments. Researchers found that students performed better when teachers expected more from them. This "Big Magic Effect" shows that setting high expectations motivates people to work harder and achieve better outcomes. Similarly, if we believe we are lucky, we are more likely to stay optimistic, seize opportunities, and achieve positive results.

Humans are inherently unsatisfied, constantly desiring more until they learn the true value of gratitude for what they already possess.

The billionaire flying in a private jet reminisces about the simplicity of the old days. The millionaire traveling in first class longs to own a private jet. The businessman driving a luxurious sports car dreams of gaining more power. The employee in an aging vehicle aspires to own a sleek, expensive car. The unemployed cyclist wishes for a stable job and a vehicle of his own. The pedestrian, weary from endless walking, hopes for a bicycle to ease his journey. The paralyzed man in a wheelchair would trade everything just to take a single step again.

And amidst it all, the terminally ill wish for nothing more than the gift of health.

Every new day brings more reasons for gratitude and joy. I am grateful for the good things in my life, both big and small, and I am excited for the abundance that is on its way. Life is full of possibilities, and I am open to receiving all the blessings that are meant for me. I trust that everything is unfolding in perfect timing, and I am fully aligned with the energy of good fortune. My heart is full of gratitude, and I welcome every blessing with open arms.

Good luck is not something that just happens to me; it is a reflection of the energy I put out into the world. I am aligned with the vibrations of success, love, happiness, and wealth. I attract opportunities that align with my highest good, and I trust that each moment is leading me toward even greater joy. I know that life is always working out in my favor, and I am constantly amazed at how easily good things flow into my life. The more I focus on the good, the better I attract, and I am becoming more and more fortunate with every passing day.

My life is truly blessed, and I am living a life filled with good luck, prosperity, and joy. As I continue to embrace the abundance that surrounds me, I remain open to all the wonderful possibilities that await me. I am a beacon of positivity, and my good luck attracts more success, more happiness, and more blessings. I am fortunate, I am lucky, and I am thankful for the amazing life that I am living.

It sounds like you're deeply focused on positive affirmations and setting intentions for good luck and success. These affirmations can certainly have a powerful impact on your mindset and confidence. If you're aiming to make the most of this energy, you could try integrating these affirmations into a daily routine, perhaps through meditation or journaling. Visualization techniques could also help amplify your expectations for positive outcomes, reinforcing that everything is always working out for you.

Is there something specific you want to focus on or achieve with these affirmations, or would you like more suggestions on how to incorporate them into your life?

• • •

Saying "I am lucky" is not just a statement of circumstance, but a conscious choice to see the world through a lens of gratitude, optimism, and possibility.

• • •

CHAPTER XIII

Mind Games- I

• • •

"The most dangerous person is the one who listens, thinks, and observes"
| Bruce Lee,Hong Kong-American martial artist and actor

• • •

The title I have chosen, **"Mind Games,"** is a fascinating topic to delve into. But what exactly do we mean by "game"? In my opinion, a game is an activity where you play with something, often for enjoyment or challenge. However, when it comes to *mind games*, the concept shifts here, the "game" involves playing with the thoughts, emotions, or perceptions of others. Mind games are about influencing, manipulating, or understanding the mental state of others, often to achieve a specific outcome. They require strategy, awareness, and a deep understanding of how the human mind operates.

It is a psychological tactics or manipulative strategies that people use to influence or control the thoughts, emotions, and behaviors of others. Often subtle and calculated, these games can take many forms, ranging from passive-aggressive comments and manipulative silence to more overt psychological tricks like gaslighting or playing on someone's fears and insecurities. The aim of mind games is typically to assert power or gain an advantage in a situation, whether it's in personal relationships, professional environments, or social interactions. They can create confusion, uncertainty, and self-doubt in the target, making them question their own perceptions, decisions, and beliefs. The person employing mind games often seeks to destabilize the other person's sense of reality, making them more dependent on the manipulator for validation or clarity.

Instead of starting a request with "could you," begin with "please." This small shift prevents the listener from perceiving your request as hypothetical, increasing their likelihood of compliance. Similarly, subtle body language, like nodding while speaking, encourages attentiveness and can sway responses in your favor. These small adjustments demonstrate how the way we frame words or gestures can impact outcomes.

In more challenging situations, such as negotiations or public speaking, staying calm and acknowledging your anxiety can work wonders. For instance, admitting nervousness while speaking can disarm tension and foster empathy from your audience. It makes you more relatable, creating a positive connection rather than resistance.

Another powerful approach is using positive reinforcement to motivate others. For example, when working with a lazy team member, praising even minor progress can inspire them to improve. Encouragement can often be more effective than criticism.

Interestingly, these techniques extend beyond interpersonal relationships. Managing your own intrusive thoughts can also be simplified using absurd strategies like repeating ridiculous phrases to shift your focus and regain calm. Such methods may sound unconventional but can be surprisingly effective in breaking cycles of anxiety or overthinking.

Mind games can also occur within the self-people may engage in negative self-talk, overthinking, or doubting their own abilities as a way to protect themselves from failure or perceived rejection. This internalized form of mind games can limit personal growth, confidence, and success, as individuals may become trapped in cycles of self-doubt and fear.

The difference between a truly intelligent person and someone who merely pretends to be intelligent lies in their approach to communication and understanding. A pretender often uses complex and difficult words in their speech, attempting to appear knowledgeable. They tend to discuss complicated topics without any first-hand experience and rely heavily on references, quoting books or papers as if reciting rehearsed material. Their conversations may sound impressive on the surface, but lack depth and genuine insight.

A truly intelligent person communicates in a simple, clear, and relatable manner. They have the ability to explain even complex topics in a way that anyone can understand. Their speech may seem modest or average, but it reflects a deep understanding of the subject. Their focus is not on impressing others, but on effectively conveying their thoughts and knowledge. True intelligence lies in clarity, not complexity, and the ability to make a meaningful connection through understanding rather than pretense.

• • •

"If you don't like a Rule...Just Follow it...Reach on the Top...And Change the Rule"
| Adolf Hitler

• • •

If you have money, rules can become flexible. If you have power, rules will serve you. But if you lack both money and power, rules are often designed to bind you. People may praise you at times, but do not let compliments sink too deeply into your heart. If you do, when they criticize you, you might begin to believe those words as well.

One day, someone who treated you poorly might suddenly become kind. Understand that this change is rarely due to regret or remorse for their actions; it is often because they need something from you. Kindness without reason is rare most acts of kindness come with an expectation of something in return. Free things are seldom truly free, and the value of generosity is often taken for granted.

Be cautious about being too generous with everyone. The more you give, the more people will expect from you, and in their greed, they may exploit your kindness. Similarly, the more you forgive someone without limits, the more they will hurt you without restraint.

You don't need too many friends in life. At times, friends can act as enemies, especially in the unpredictable game of life. Guard your trust, set boundaries, and prioritize self-respect over the fleeting approval of others.

Understanding human behavior is essential if you want to navigate relationships, influence others, and position yourself as a person of value. One fundamental truth is this: **arguing rarely earns your respect.** Instead, it alienates people, annoys them, and often ostracizes you.

The better approach? **Show results.** Let your actions speak louder than your words. People respect results because they are tangible, undeniable, and far more persuasive than verbal battles.

But earning respect is only part of the equation. To truly master influence, you must also understand how to manage perceptions, project power, and maintain your value in others' eyes.

• • •

The Game of Perception

Power isn't just about what you possess; it's about how others perceive you. In the game of life, **perception is power.** People will judge you based on how you present yourself not necessarily on who you are at your core.

To project power effectively, focus on these key principles:

1. **Create a Powerful Image:**

   ◦ Dress well. Appear confident. Speak with clarity and purpose.
   ◦ Align yourself with individuals, ideas, or causes that others admire. Associating yourself with something greater can amplify your perceived value.

2. **Leverage Perception to Your Advantage:**

- The way others see you can often be more influential than your actual abilities. This doesn't mean being deceptive but rather being intentional about how you present yourself.
- Focus on showcasing your strengths and minimizing your weaknesses in public.

Remember the saying:

"Even the smallest person can cast a large shadow

• • •

• • •

The Utility of Being Useful

Another truth about human relationships is this: **people value you as long as you are useful to them.**

This may sound harsh, but it's a fundamental aspect of human nature. When you are seen as someone who contributes value whether through your skills, resources, or connections people will respect and rely on you. But the moment you stop being useful, their perception of you diminishes.

To maintain your value:

1. **Always Offer Something of Value:**

Continuously improve yourself, acquire new skills, and stay relevant in your circle. If you're always growing, you'll always have something to offer.

2. **Avoid Creating Self-Sufficient Competitors:**

Teaching and helping others are noble, but be mindful of how much you share. If you teach someone everything you know, to the point where they become self-sufficient and no longer need you, your value in their eyes may decrease.

Instead, maintain a balance:

- ○ Empower others, but keep certain skills or knowledge exclusive to yourself.
- ○ Ensure that your contributions are indispensable.

As the saying goes:

"Power is not about how strong you are it's about how strong people believe you are."

• • •

If you want to increase your value, start by being less available. When you constantly make yourself accessible to everyone, your time and presence begin to lose their worth. People naturally take for granted what they can have anytime, and being overly available often leads to a lack of appreciation or even disrespect. Just as gold is highly valued because of its rarity, your value rises when your attention and presence are not so easily given. When you're always there, people may start to see you as someone who has nothing important going on, which diminishes how they perceive you.

Instead, shift your focus to building your own life, pursuing your goals, and working on your personal growth. Fill your time with meaningful activities that show you value yourself. This doesn't mean being cold or distant, but rather creating healthy boundaries and making your time feel like a privilege, not a given. By doing so, you create a space that allows others to realize your worth, and they'll begin to appreciate and respect the moments they do get with you.

Absence can often be more powerful than presence. When you're not always available, people will naturally start to value you more because they'll recognize what they're missing. Your limited availability makes your interactions more meaningful and impactful, while also ensuring that you're not wasting time on people who don't genuinely value you. Respect isn't demanded it's earned through the way you carry yourself. By protecting your time, you not only gain respect but also make room for the right people who truly appreciate your presence.

In essence, prioritize yourself and your goals first. When you get busy with your life and stop offering unlimited access to your time, you'll naturally gain respect and elevate your value in the eyes of others. People will always chase what feels exclusive, so be the person who values their time and energy enough to give it sparingly.

We naturally gravitate towards and trust those who maintain a steady, resilient presence, especially during difficult times. Look at the people in your life those friends or acquaintances who, despite facing personal struggles, continue to show up with strength and positivity. Whether it's going through a painful breakup, dealing with financial challenges, recovering from a failed exam, or enduring setbacks that many would consider crushing, they don't let these external circumstances alter their inner state. They continue to navigate life with calmness, clarity, and a sense of purpose. This ability to remain composed and focused, no matter what life throws at them, is what sets them apart as true leaders.

These people don't react impulsively or let their emotions spiral when things go wrong. Instead, they manage their internal world and remain grounded, even when the external world seems chaotic. It's their inner stability that attracts others and makes them trustworthy in moments of crisis. They may not have all the answers or perfect solutions, but they have something more valuable: the capacity to handle adversity without losing themselves in it. Their strength doesn't lie in their ability to avoid pain or failure, but in their ability to confront it head-on and keep moving forward.

True leadership is not about being immune to struggle or never experiencing hardship. It's about showing others how to respond when life challenges you. The person who can remain calm, centered, and clear-headed in the face of adversity inspires others to do the same. They demonstrate that real leadership comes from within through emotional intelligence, resilience, and the ability to maintain peace of mind, regardless of the circumstances. This is what attracts others, what creates trust, and what defines a leader.

You can read people like an open book by observing their body language and the subtle signals they send through their posture and gestures. For example, people who sit with their arms folded often have strong, determined personalities and a powerful attitude. However, it's important to note that this posture should feel natural, not forced, because arms folded can also signal a defensive stance, as if the person is guarding themselves or protecting their inner thoughts. Similarly, when someone touches their chin while speaking, it usually indicates self-reflection or caution. They might be carefully considering their words or are hesitant about making a mistake. It suggests that they are being thoughtful, weighing their options before speaking.

On the other hand, constant laughter, especially when someone laughs at everything, could be a sign of deeper sadness or emotional struggle that they are hiding. If you notice this, don't ignore it ask if everything is okay in their life. Lighten the mood with friendly conversation, perhaps even jokingly asking, "Why are you smiling so much are you hiding something?" This approach could help ease their discomfort and show that you care. Lastly, when someone sits with their arms crossed over their chest, it typically means they have strong opinions and are protective of their views. While this can indicate confidence, it can also point to stubbornness or a defensive mechanism, where they feel the need to shield themselves from criticism or judgment. Understanding these small but powerful body cues can provide insight into a person's emotions and mindset, allowing you to connect with them more meaningfully.

I believe that if you think you can't achieve something, then you're right you won't. Your mindset is everything, and having a positive attitude can completely change your reality. The human mind has untapped potential that most people don't fully utilize. It's said that humans only use about 1% of their mental capacity, leaving 99% untapped. If we could unlock even a fraction of that unused potential, we could accomplish extraordinary things. Our minds are capable of incredible feats, from solving major problems to curing diseases, yet most people don't realize just how powerful they truly are. The key lies in cultivating the right mindset, pushing beyond limitations, and believing in the vast potential within you. By doing so, you can begin to tap into that unused 99% and unlock the greatness you are capable of achieving.

If you want to buy something, don't focus solely on the price tag. Instead, think about the value it brings to your life. Make decisions without constantly looking at the clock or worrying about the cost, but rather consider whether the purchase is something that will truly enrich your life in the long run. Sometimes, it's important to prioritize quality, experience, or long-term benefits over immediate price concerns. When you shift your focus from the cost to the value, you make choices that align with your true needs and desires.

• • •

"Act like the person you want to become, no matter how you feel right now."
| Mel Robbins, American presenter and author

• • •

Power of the Mind: Be Like Water, Shape Your Thoughts
Bruce Lee once said, *"Be formless, shapeless, like water. Empty your mind, be formless. Water can flow, or it can crash."* This profound philosophy teaches us about the true nature of our mind and thoughts. Just like water, our mind is fluid it flows effortlessly, adapting to its environment. Water has no fixed shape; it takes the form of whatever container it occupies. Similarly, our thoughts are dynamic, often uncontrollable, and constantly changing.

Many philosophies and scientific studies emphasize that our mind resembles water because of its adaptability and unpredictability. Our thoughts can be calm and slow like a still lake, or fast and turbulent like a rushing river. This fluid nature of the mind makes it difficult to control, and overthinking becomes a natural byproduct. Interestingly, even biologically, the brain is made up of approximately 15% water, which further reflects its fluidity and connection to this metaphor.

However, while we may not be able to fully control our thoughts, we can guide and shape them. Just as water takes the shape of the container it is poured into; our thoughts can be given direction and purpose. For instance, imagine lying on your bed, feeling lazy, and someone asks you to move a heavy box to the storage room. In that moment, your mind will perceive the task as burdensome and you'll likely feel resistant. But if someone instead asks you to lift the same box during a workout session at the gym, you would likely approach the task with enthusiasm and energy.

By understanding and embracing the nature of your mind as formless and fluid, you can learn to shape it to your advantage. Like water, your thoughts have immense potential they can nourish and create, or they can flood and overwhelm. The choice lies in how you guide them.

So, empty your mind, be like water, and let your thoughts flow with purpose. Once you master the art of shaping your thoughts, you'll find that you can achieve clarity, focus, and a sense of inner peace. Let your mind flow where you want it to go, and watch as you transform challenges into opportunities and dreams into reality.

The distinction between the rich and the poor is not merely about wealth; it is deeply rooted in mindset, priorities, and choices. A rich man knows the value of focus and avoids distractions. He doesn't waste time indulging in meaningless pursuits. Instead, he channels his energy into developing skills that enhance his value and open doors to greater opportunities. On the other hand, a poor man often spends his limited resources on distractions, entertainment, and fleeting pleasures rather than investing in skills that could lead to lasting success.

Time is another crucial factor. A rich man understands that time is his most precious asset, so he buys it. He delegates tasks, uses his time productively, and focuses on activities that drive growth and wealth creation. In contrast, a poor man often sells his time, exchanging hours for minimal pay, rarely considering how to leverage his efforts for greater rewards. This mindset traps him in a cycle of survival rather than growth.

The rich also prioritize growth over comfort. They invest in personal development, education, businesses, and ventures that yield exponential returns. Growth requires effort, discipline, and a willingness to step out of one's comfort zone. Meanwhile, the poor often prioritize comfort, spending their money and time on short-term pleasures and maintaining a lifestyle that offers immediate gratification but no progress. This difference in priorities creates a widening gap between the two mindsets.

Distractions are another defining factor. A rich man guards his focus, understanding that distractions whether from social media, entertainment, or unnecessary commitments can derail progress. The poor, however, often fall prey to these distractions, allowing their time and energy to be consumed by things that do not contribute to their goals or growth. This inability to focus on what truly matters keeps them from achieving the success they desire.

The rich think long-term. They are willing to make sacrifices today for a better tomorrow, seeing the bigger picture and planning for years or even decades ahead. The poor, however, tend to think short-term, focusing on immediate needs and pleasures without considering how their choices today will impact their future. This short-sightedness often leads to missed opportunities and stagnant growth.

To bridge this gap, one must make a conscious effort to shift their mindset. Instead of seeking temporary pleasures, focus on building skills and knowledge that can create lasting value. Instead of wasting time on distractions, channel your energy into meaningful pursuits that align with your long-term goals. Growth demands effort, discipline, and the courage to leave your comfort zone behind.

Success is not an accident. It is the result of deliberate choices and consistent actions. The difference between the rich and the poor lies not in their circumstances but in their ability to think differently, prioritize growth, and focus on long-term success.

Change your mindset today, and you'll change your life tomorrow.

• • •

"You never attract what you want in your life, you only attract who you are"
| Bob Proctor, Canadian author

• • •

The Raven and the Eagle: A Story of Power and Success
In the world of the wild, there is a quiet truth: those who remain weak and dependent will always be exploited. It's a harsh rule, but it's the reality for those who lack strength or independence. Take the story of the raven and the eagle, for example. The eagle, known as the king of birds, is powerful and unyielding. He soars high in the sky, taking the meat from the lion's mouth such is his dominance that even the mighty lion runs at the sound of his call. But there's a raven that follows the eagle, perched on his back, living off the eagle's strength, traveling the skies with him.

The eagle climbs higher and higher, reaching altitudes where the air grows thin, and oxygen levels begin to decrease. As the heights increase, the raven starts to struggle. It becomes harder to breathe, and the raven is forced to leave the eagle's back. The eagle, in his strength and power, can continue soaring, unaffected by the challenges of altitude.

This story serves as a powerful metaphor for life. Just as the raven clung to the eagle, we too often find ourselves dependent on others, relying on their strength to carry us. But as we grow in power, as we increase our success and elevate ourselves, those who once relied on us or sought to bring us down will find themselves suffocating. Like the raven, they cannot rise to the heights we've reached. They become weighed down by their own limitations, while we continue to soar, unburdened.

The true lesson is this: the key to overcoming dependence and exploitation is to rise higher not just in terms of material wealth or physical stature, but in power, wisdom, and success. When you elevate yourself in these areas, you leave behind the constraints that once held you down, and those who try to defeat you will find that the higher you go, the more difficult it becomes for them to reach you.

$\bullet\ \bullet\ \bullet$

Study war, but read poetry.
Understand science, but discover art.

$\bullet\ \bullet\ \bullet$

For example, if you want to burn a piece of paper using a magnifying glass, you must focus the sunlight on a single spot for some time. Even though the sun is incredibly powerful and vast, it cannot burn the paper without the concentrated focus provided by the magnifying glass. This illustrates an important life lesson: instead of spreading your energy across too many things, focus on one goal or skill and dedicate yourself to mastering it. Just as the focused sunlight ignites the paper, concentrated effort and attention can lead to remarkable success in your chosen pursuit.

The Wisdom of Discretion and Self-Protection

In life, it's important to recognize the value of discretion. If your salary is $105,000 and you tell your family it's $40,000, and to outsiders, it's $15,000 or $20,000, you're not being honest you're simply protecting your privacy. This isn't about lying; it's about knowing when and to whom you reveal details. The truth is, people often reveal too much too quickly, believing that transparency is always a virtue. But this can be foolishness. It opens doors for others to take advantage of your personal information, and once it's out there, you can't take it back.

Similarly, when it comes to offering advice, be careful. Even though you may have good intentions, you're not always guaranteed credit for your wisdom. If the advice fails, you'll be the one blamed, and that's a position no one wants to be in.

At a party or in a social setting, if you don't want to be the center of attention or have your personal matters discussed, avoid mentioning sensitive topics. For instance, discussing a doctor or personal issues could invite unwanted probing from people who don't have your best interests at heart.

Some people will deliberately put you in awkward positions, trying to manipulate or control the conversation to their advantage. It's essential to recognize these tactics early and stay away from those who try to push you into uncomfortable situations. You don't need to be overly accommodating to everyone, and it's okay to keep some things to yourself.

In life, how you are treated by others often reflects how you should treat them in return. If someone treats you as an option, offering you only fleeting attention when it's convenient for them, it's crucial to understand that you deserve more than that. In such cases, it's only wise to make them an option in your life as well. You don't need to chase after someone who doesn't prioritize you; instead, shift your focus to those who recognize your value and invest in your relationship.

On the other hand, when someone treats you as a choice when they genuinely consider your feelings, show you respect, and make space for you in their life then they deserve to be seen as the brand in your life. Just as a brand carry meaning, loyalty, and trust, the person who values you should hold a prominent and cherished place in your world. They become not just a part of your life, but a symbol of what true respect and care look like.

This dynamic is all about self-respect and mutual respect. You should never settle for being an option, nor should you ever treat someone else as just another choice. By recognizing and fostering relationships where both parties are equally valued, you create a life built on strong, meaningful connections that enrich and empower you.

In life, we all have insecurities whether it's about our height, our eyes, our hair, or something else. We may not openly admit it, but deep down, those little vulnerabilities can affect how we see ourselves. When someone makes even a small comment about something we're insecure about, like our height, it feels like a sharp reminder of the wound we've been carrying. It stings because we already know there's something we're sensitive about, and that comment only brings it to the surface.

However, the key to no longer letting these comments bother you is simple: full self-acceptance. When you truly accept yourself flaws and all those external opinions lose their power. It's not about being perfect or flawless; it's about embracing who you are, as you are, without constantly seeking validation from others. Once you reach that point of self-acceptance, the opinions of others become irrelevant because you've already recognized your worth and your uniqueness.

Of course, this doesn't mean you shouldn't work on areas you want to improve. Accepting yourself doesn't mean complacency; it means acknowledging what you can change and taking active steps to grow. Whether it's physical, emotional, or mental improvement, focusing on what you can enhance while accepting your current self will allow you to live confidently, unaffected by others' judgments. When you accept yourself fully, nothing anyone says will ever shake your sense of self-worth.

An angry mind is a narrow mind. When you allow anger to take over, it clouds your judgment and limits your ability to think clearly. In those moments of frustration, all you can focus on is what the other person did or what you want to do to them. You're consumed by emotions, and it's easy to forget that anger doesn't solve anything it only escalates the situation. Instead of thinking rationally about the potential consequences of your actions, anger narrows your perspective, pushing you to react impulsively.

Anger often makes us feel like we're working harder or that we're in control, but in reality, it's only burning out our minds. The energy you invest in anger is draining and destructive, leaving you exhausted and regretful. The body follows the mind, so when your thoughts are consumed by anger, your actions are likely to follow the same destructive path. It's an exhausting cycle that never leads to a positive outcome.

In contrast, when you remain calm, you open yourself up to strategic thinking. Instead of allowing your opponent to control your emotions, you take charge. Sometimes, the best way to control a situation is by staying composed, knowing that by keeping your cool, you can make the other person angry, which clouds their judgment and makes them more vulnerable to your influence. By mastering your emotions, you maintain control, leaving your opponent to lose theirs. In the battle of minds, calmness is the true strength.

Believing in someone else's wisdom or perspective without fully understanding it yourself can be dangerous. It's like poisoning your own intelligence, letting someone else's beliefs overshadow your own. The truth is, you don't need to blindly believe in anyone, including me. While advice can guide you, your true path can only be discovered by trusting your own insights, your inner voice. It's essential to find your own direction and follow it with conviction, no matter where it leads you.

The path you walk is yours and yours alone. The question isn't whether others are following the same path it's about whether that path is right for you. Every individual's journey is unique, and it's in that uniqueness that the true beauty of life lies. We are all different, and that's what makes each of our stories powerful. Embrace your individuality and trust that the insights you discover within yourself will lead you to where you are meant to be. The key to growth and fulfillment is not in following others, but in courageously walking your own path.

Human psychology is complex, and one of its more subtle truths is that no one likes to feel overshadowed. When someone perceives you as better or more successful than them, it can breed feelings of envy. Envy, left unchecked, can lead to destructive behavior. People who are envious of you may try to damage your reputation, degrade you with hurtful words, or entangle you in situations meant to bring you down. They may not appear as threats, but their intentions are rooted in insecurity and jealousy.

Life is already filled with challenges and obstacles, and when you encounter envy, it creates unnecessary, additional hurdles. The key to dealing with envy is to remain calm and composed, even when faced with jealousy or negativity. Keep your attitude grounded and humble. Those who wish to bring you down through envy will be disarmed by your quiet confidence and humility. Instead of seeing you as a threat, they will come to respect you for the way you handle adversity.

By staying true to yourself and not reacting to their negativity, you shift the power back into your hands. Your calmness will send a message that you are not intimidated, and over time, even the most envious individuals will learn to respect you. In the face of envy, the best response is not aggression, but quiet strength and humility. This approach not only defuses hostility but also helps you continue your growth without unnecessary distractions.

There is immense value in doing things quietly and strategically. The most successful individuals often operate behind the scenes, building quietly, investing wisely, and acting with intention. Instead of broadcasting your every move, make your decisions in silence. Buy property discreetly, plan significant events on auspicious dates, and when the time comes, reveal them only when everything is in place. Whether it's proposing to someone or throwing a wedding, doing so privately and then inviting others only to the celebration adds an element of surprise and respect for the process.

Life, much like a game of chess, is about making moves that are deliberate and thoughtful. In chess, players only announce "checkmate" when their strategy has been executed successfully. Similarly, life is not about revealing your vision to others prematurely, only to face skepticism or unnecessary distractions. It's about quietly working toward your goal and making your impact felt when the time is right. By holding back from sharing your plans before they're fully formed, you maintain focus and avoid attracting unwanted attention that could derail your progress.

Sometimes, the most powerful things are done without fanfare. The less you talk about your ambitions, the more energy you can direct toward achieving them. Let your actions speak louder than your words. When you do this, you create a sense of mystery and respect around your intentions, allowing you to move with clarity, avoid unnecessary judgment, and ultimately, achieve your vision.

Turning Enemies into Friends: The Benjamin Franklin Effect

In 1740, Benjamin Franklin employed a simple yet powerful psychological strategy to transform a rival into an ally. He borrowed a book from a legislator who strongly disliked him. After returning it with a gracious thank-you note, Franklin noticed a significant shift in the rival's attitude. The once-hostile man began treating him with warmth and respect. But why did this happen?

This phenomenon, now known as the *Benjamin Franklin Effect*, occurs because when someone does a favor for us, they subconsciously begin to justify their actions by developing a more positive attitude toward us. Our minds strive for consistency when we extend kindness, our emotions naturally align to support that behavior. By doing a favor, the person convinces themselves that they must have had a good reason for helping, thus fostering genuine goodwill.

The more favors people do for us, the stronger their positive feelings grow. The best way to win over an adversary is not through confrontation, but through subtle acts of engagement and trust.

Have you ever imagined possessing the power to change someone? People often believe they can transform others, but the truth is, you cannot force anyone to change. Change is a deeply personal journey no one will change simply because you want them to.

One of the greatest barriers to change is the human ego. When people feel challenged or criticized, they instinctively defend themselves, protecting their pride. No one wants to feel weak or inadequate. That is why simply telling someone they are wrong or trying to impose your beliefs will only make them resist even more.

True influence lies not in proving someone wrong but in showing them their untapped potential. People don't change because they are told to they change when they see for themselves what they are truly capable of. When you inspire others to recognize the greatness within them, they no longer feel threatened by change; instead, they embrace it. They don't transform for your sake, but because they finally understand what they were meant for. Real change happens when you help people see the extraordinary within themselves.

The Power of Price Anchoring in Business

In business, the way you present your products or services can significantly influence customer decisions. One effective strategy is called price anchoring, which involves setting a reference point for customers by initially presenting them with a higher-priced option. Let's say you're selling a car worth $20,000. Instead of starting with the $20,000 car, you first show them a more expensive model, say one priced at $30,000 or $40,000. When customers see the higher-priced option, they're likely to perceive the $20,000 car as more reasonable and affordable in comparison, even though it's still the same price.

This technique works because humans tend to make decisions relative to the information available to them. The initial exposure to a more expensive product serves as an "anchor" for their expectations, making the $20,000 car seem like a much better deal. When the expensive car feels out of reach, the $20,000 option suddenly appears to be a more sensible and affordable choice.

Price anchoring taps into the psychology of perception and helps customers feel like they're making a smarter, more economical decision. It shifts their perspective and makes the price of the product you actually want to sell seem more attractive by comparison. This strategy can be applied in various industries whether in retail, real estate, or even services were offering a higher-priced item first can set the stage for a more favorable perception of your primary offering.

In today's world, what is visible often holds more value than quality. People are drawn to what they can see, what looks appealing, while the true essence or quality may be overlooked. This reflects the notion that perception often outweighs reality. I am reminded of the saying, "Gaging is fate's rule in the palace, and spectacle is revered in the streets." It suggests that while the elite or those in power may rely on status and appearances to define their world, in the public eye, it is spectacle and showmanship that command attention and admiration. Ultimately, what is seen often trumps what is real, and the outward display becomes the measure of worth.

The Power of Perception in Decision-Making

Imagine you need to undergo surgery. Would you choose a doctor with a 90% success rate or one with a 10% failure rate? Most people instinctively prefer the doctor with the higher success rate. But here's the truth both doctors are equally skilled. The difference lies not in their abilities but in how the information is presented.

This phenomenon highlights the power of framing. When success is emphasized, people feel reassured and confident in their choice. However, when failure is brought into focus, fear and doubt creep in. The same reality can be perceived in vastly different ways depending on how it is communicated.

Framing influences not only our decisions but also our emotions and perceptions. Whether positive or negative, the way information is presented can shape our understanding, often without us even realizing it. Recognizing this cognitive bias allows us to make more rational, informed decisions rather than being swayed by the way facts are framed.

The Weight of Fixing Someone: A Lesson in Love

It's natural to want to erase the pain of someone you love. You see their struggles, their wounds, and you feel a deep desire to heal them, to make them whole again. But what many don't realize is that when you're trying to fix someone, you're not just dealing with the person in front of you you're dealing with their past, their childhood, and the scars left by years of hurt and trauma.

Some people carry a hollow space within themselves, a void created by past pain. They may have convinced themselves, because of what they've endured, that no one can truly love them or that everyone who does will eventually leave. If you love someone like this, you might find yourself pouring all your energy into trying to prove them wrong, trying to heal their broken pieces. But in the process, you risk losing yourself. You become a therapist instead of a partner, and that dynamic rarely leads to happiness for either of you.

True love isn't about fixing someone. It's about mutual respect, support, and growth. If someone's pain is so consuming that it begins to drain you, the kindest thing you can do for both of you is to step back. Wish them well, hope for their healing, and let them walk their journey on their own. Your love and energy are precious, and they deserve to be given to someone who values them, someone who can meet you halfway.

You can't save everyone. And sometimes, the best way to love someone is to let them go so they can learn to save themselves.

• • •

"When fishermen cannot go to sea, they repair their nets"
| Steve Jobs, Former CEO of Apple

• • •

The Power of Imperfection: The Prattfall Effect

Did you know that making small, harmless mistakes can actually make you more attractive? In 1966, a social psychologist conducted a fascinating study known as the *Pratfall Effect*. The research revealed that people who occasionally make small blunders like dropping something while walking or accidentally leaving a tag on their clothes are often perceived as more likable and approachable than those who seem flawless.

Why does this happen? The answer lies in relatability. When someone appears too perfect, it can create a sense of distance or even intimidation. But when they reveal a small, human flaw, it breaks the illusion of perfection and makes them feel more genuine and relatable. These minor missteps show others that you're just like them imperfect, real, and down-to-earth.

This doesn't mean you should go out of your way to make mistakes, but it's a gentle reminder that perfection isn't always the goal. In fact, embracing your small quirks and flaws can make you even more endearing. People are drawn to authenticity, not perfection. So, the next time you trip over your words or drop your coffee, don't be embarrassed those little moments might just make you more magnetic than you realize.

The Power of a King's Mindset

A slave remains a slave, and a king remains a king not because of their circumstances, but because of their mindset. If you were to hand a kingdom to a slave, they would likely lose it in no time. But if you were to send a true king into an unknown land, even with nothing, he would eventually build a new kingdom from the ground up.

Why? Because a king's vision and approach to life are fundamentally different. A king sees a sword as a weapon to conquer, while a slave might only see it as a tool for survival. A king looks beyond the present, planning for the future, while a slave often remains focused on the immediate. It's not about their current status it's about their mindset, their foresight, and their ability to see the bigger picture.

This principle applies to life as well. If your vision is small, even opportunities of great value will slip through your hands. But when you think like a king when you adopt a long-term, strategic mindset no obstacle can stop you. You understand that building something meaningful takes time, yet you remain steadfast, knowing that success is inevitable with effort and focus.

So, whether you're building a career, a business, or a legacy, cultivate the mindset of a king. Think big, plan ahead, and never limit your vision to the present moment. A $100 product becomes priceless when it's part of a larger vision. Build with intention, lead with wisdom, and success will follow.

The saddest people on Earth are those who are both ambitious and lazy. They dream of achieving great things, yet their unwillingness to put in the necessary effort holds them back. Their ambition fills them with desires and aspirations, but their laziness chains them to inaction, creating a constant state of frustration and regret. These individuals live with the burden of untapped potential, watching opportunities slip away simply because they lack the discipline to act. Ambition without effort is like a ship without a sail it has the capacity to go far but remains adrift, going nowhere. True fulfillment comes when ambition is matched with hard work and perseverance.

Hunt or to be hunted

The hunter must always be prepared to become the hunted. This simple truth reflects the cycle of power, survival, and consequence. In the wild, a predator hunts to sustain itself, but it is never exempt from the risk of being hunted in return. This idea extends beyond nature to life itself those who pursue power, dominance, or success must also be vigilant, as their actions can invite challenges or threats from others. "Hunt to be hunted" serves as a reminder that no position is ever absolute, and the balance of life often demands both caution and humility.

Once upon a time, in a dense jungle, there lived a lion. One day, the lion noticed a strange smell coming from his body. Curious and wanting to confirm this, he approached a deer and asked, "Do I smell strange to you?" Without thinking, the deer truthfully replied, "Yes, you do." The lion, offended and enraged by the deer's blunt response, killed the deer in his anger.

Later, the lion encountered a monkey and asked him the same question. The monkey, terrified of the lion, nervously replied, "Oh no, my lord, you smell perfectly fine. You are the mighty lion!" However, the lion sensed the monkey's fear and dishonesty, so he killed the monkey as well.

Finally, the lion approached a fox and repeated his question: "Do I smell strange to you?" The clever fox, understanding the gravity of the situation, tactfully responded, "My lord, you smell as fresh and regal as ever! However, I have a cold and cannot fully trust my sense of smell at the moment." The lion, satisfied with this diplomatic answer, left the fox unharmed.

Moral of the story: Not every question requires a direct answer, especially if it serves no purpose or leads to trouble. Sometimes, it is wiser to avoid unnecessary conflicts and meaningless conversations. Diplomacy and tact can often save the day.

Act like you can't afford the bread until they discover you own the entire bakery. The importance of humility, even when you hold great power, success, or wealth. In a world often obsessed with outward displays of status, staying grounded and unassuming allows your true worth to shine when the time is right. Let your actions and achievements speak louder than any boastful words. Humility is not about denying your success it's about carrying it with grace. Remember, the most impactful individuals are those who remain humble, no matter how high they rise.

Think about it what holds greater significance for you: an empty stomach or respect? Which is more essential in your life? Many people advise that where you are not respected, you should not remain. In that sense, respect seems to hold a higher value than satisfying an empty stomach. But is it truly so?

You may believe that giving respect is more valuable than offering food. You may feel honored when someone bestows respect upon you, but in reality, that person may be subtly bending you down under the weight of their acknowledgment. Respect, when given with ulterior motives, can be a tool of manipulation rather than a token of honor.

So, whenever someone offers you respect, pause and reflect is it genuine, or is it a carefully laid trap? Sometimes, respect is not a gift but a siren's call, luring you into a web of influence and control.

No one can harm iron; it is only rust that weakens and destroys it from within. Similarly, people cannot be harmed by others unless they allow negative thoughts, doubts, or fears to take root in their minds. Just as rust is created by the reaction of iron to its surroundings, a person's own thoughts can become their greatest enemy. It is a reminder that external factors are rarely as powerful as the strength or weakness within us. Guard your mind, for it holds the key to your resilience and well-being.

The interesting fact about the rat race is that even if you win, you're still a rat. The endless cycle of competition and striving for material success in today's world. People often chase after wealth, status, and recognition, believing that victory in this race will bring fulfillment. However, the reality is that the rat race traps individuals in a system where true freedom and happiness are elusive. Winning the race may give temporary satisfaction, but it doesn't change the nature of the race itself or the constraints it imposes. True success lies in stepping out of the race altogether, pursuing a life of purpose, balance, and self-awareness instead of mindless competition.

It is not always the strongest who win, but rather those who understand the rules. Success in life is less about brute strength and more about strategy, adaptability, and wisdom. Knowing the rules whether they are the unspoken norms of society, the laws of nature, or the principles of any game gives you the advantage to navigate challenges effectively. Strength alone can only take you so far, but understanding how to play the game allows you to turn even the smallest opportunities into great victories. True winners are those who combine intelligence, patience, and awareness to outthink and outmaneuver their competition.

The true value of medicine is not recognized before an accident but becomes undeniably clear after one. This reflects a broader truth about life: we often overlook the importance of things until we need them the most. Just as medicine might seem insignificant when we're healthy, it's worth becomes priceless in moments of crisis. This teaches us to value things our health, relationships, and even preventative care before circumstances force us to realize their significance. Preparedness and gratitude for what we have can save us from regret later, much like understanding the importance of medicine before it's urgently needed.

The value of time can only be truly understood by those who feel its impact the most. Ask the value of one year to a student who has failed their exams, and they will tell you how precious it is. Ask the value of one month to a pregnant woman eagerly awaiting the arrival of her child, and she will show you its worth. Ask the value of one week to the editor of a newspaper, racing against deadlines to deliver the news, and they will explain its importance. Ask the value of one day to a prisoner who is set to be executed tomorrow, and you will see the weight it carries. Ask the value of one hour to a couple who is parting ways after a brief but cherished meeting, and they will tell you how priceless it feels. Finally, ask the value of one second to the person who missed their train by a heartbeat, and they will reveal just how significant even a moment can be.

Time is not just a measure of life emit is life itself. Every moment matters, and its value depends on the perspective of those who live it.

If you want to take revenge on a middle-class person, place them in the company of the wealthy. This is a subtle yet effective form of retribution, as it highlights the vast differences in lifestyle, values, and expectations. A middle-class person, accustomed to a simpler and more modest way of life, may find themselves overwhelmed and out of place in an environment dominated by luxury and excess. The pressure to conform to a world they are not familiar with can lead to feelings of inadequacy, frustration, and alienation.

This kind of "revenge" is not about direct confrontation or physical harm but rather about creating a sense of discomfort and disempowerment. It reveals the stark reality of how society's class divisions can affect individuals' sense of self-worth and belonging. However, it also serves as a reminder that true happiness and fulfillment do not come from wealth or status but from inner peace, self-acceptance, and the quality of relationships one cultivates.

If you find yourself lacking in hard work and determination, take a ride in the general compartment of a train. There, you will witness people from all walks of life, struggling, hustling, and persevering to reach their destinations despite the discomfort and chaos around them. It serves as a reminder of the strength and resilience that lies within human effort.

Similarly, if you feel entangled in life's problems and overwhelmed by your challenges, visit the general ward of a hospital. There, you will see individuals fighting battles far greater than your own fighting for their health, their lives, and their loved ones. It puts your struggles into perspective, teaching you to be grateful for what you have and to approach life with renewed strength.

Both experiences are profound in their own way, reminding us of the importance of hard work, resilience, and gratitude. Sometimes, a simple shift in perspective is all we need to realign ourselves with our goals and values.

How to Identify a Fake Person from a Real One

One simple way to distinguish a fake person from a real one is by observing their circle of friends. A fake person often surrounds themselves with a large group of friends, seeking attention and validation from as many people as possible. Their relationships are usually superficial, built on convenience or appearances rather than genuine connection.

In contrast, a real person typically has a smaller, close-knit circle of friends. They prioritize quality over quantity, valuing deeper, meaningful relationships over fleeting interactions. Their friendships are built on trust, loyalty, and mutual respect, rather than the need to impress others.

You cannot truly defeat a person without first breaking their will their inner drive to keep moving forward. A man's final and ultimate freedom lies in his willingness to act, to persevere despite adversity. No force, no hardship, and no external power can truly conquer someone who refuses to surrender their will. As long as the spirit remains unbroken, true defeat is impossible.

Understanding the dynamics of mind games is essential for protecting oneself from being manipulated or controlled. Setting clear boundaries, maintaining open communication, and practicing self-awareness are key to resisting these tactics. It's also important to recognize when mind games are at play and to seek support or guidance if necessary. Whether in personal or professional contexts, breaking free from mind games requires mental clarity, emotional resilience, and a commitment to healthy, honest interactions. The ability to recognize and resist mind games is crucial for fostering healthy relationships, maintaining emotional well-being, and achieving a sense of personal empowerment.

CHAPTER XIV

The First Step to Success

As the saying goes, a king's son often becomes the new king, and a politician's son often follows in their footsteps. But what about you? The truth is, you are not born into those families, nor are you putting in the necessary effort to achieve what you desire. Without relentless determination and consistent efforts, there are no other options. Your destiny lies not in the family you were born into, but in the choices, you make and the hard work you invest. Success is not a birthright; it is earned through perseverance and dedication.

The Dual Nature of Success and Failure

If you plant the seed of optimism, you must be prepared to harvest the crop of disappointment. Optimism fuels ambition, but with great expectations often come setbacks. Disappointments are not failures; they are the natural byproducts of striving for something greater.

Success is not a straight path it requires resilience and the willingness to descend into the depths of struggle. If you wish to rise high, you must first be willing to go deep, just as a well must be dug before it can provide water. True victory is not a fixed state; it is forged in the fire of repeated defeats. Only those who embrace hardship and learn from their failures can truly claim triumph.

• • •

"Ever tried Ever failed No matter, try again Fail again Fail better the world is yours Treat everyone kindly and light up the night"
| Peter Dinklage, American actor

• • •

What is the true definition of success? Does it mean earning money, or is it about being happy? Who defines success me, you, or society? The truth is, success holds a different meaning for every individual. For some, it might be achieving their goals, while for others, it might be finding joy in the journey toward those goals. In our society, success is often measured by physical and materialistic possessions such as cars, homes, gold, or wealth. But does acquiring these things truly mean you've fulfilled your life? The answer lies within each of us, and no one else can define it for you. Success is a deeply personal journey; you are your own guide, you are your own god, and your own pathfinder. You must seek your own definition and pursue it with determination.

In my opinion, success is not just about earning money or being perpetually happy or sad. Life always offers you choices to achieve what you desire, but what you choose to pursue depends entirely on you whether it is money or something else, the decision is yours. It's important to remember that while earning money may seem straightforward, managing it wisely is a far more challenging task. Success is not about flaunting your achievements to society. Often, people work hard simply to show the world they are successful, but in doing so, they become bound by society's expectations, losing sight of their true purpose.

True success comes when you free yourself from societal pressures and materialistic attachments. It is not about conforming to what society deems successful but about finding fulfillment within the process of your work. Success lies in the effort, the growth, and the meaning you derive from your journey. It's not about the destination, nor about the approval of others, but about living authentically and embracing the process of self-discovery and purpose. Let success be defined not by external standards but by the depth of contentment and freedom you experience along the way.

If you can't be better, work harder. If working harder isn't an option, choose an easier game. If an easier game isn't available, find a better partner. If you struggle to find a better partner, seek an untouched market.

There is always a way forward.

• • •

Study like there's no tomorrow-because there might not be.
Study like you're racing against time-because you are.
Study like success is a limited offer because it is.
Study like you're the only one who can change your
future-because you are.
Study like every second counts-because it does.

• • •

There are only five ways to get rich, and that's the simple truth:

1. **You have to be poor** – A poor person can only make many or if you are already financially stable and want to increase your wealth then this chapter is helpful for you, if you're rich then this chapter is not for you.
2. **Inheritance** – You're born into wealth, and your parents pass it down. It's the easiest path, but it's also the one you have no control over. Either you're lucky, or you're not.
3. **Stealing** – Whether it's through unethical shortcuts or outright crime, some choose this path. But what's stolen rarely lasts, and the cost is often your integrity or worse, your freedom.
4. **Working Hard** – The most honest and sustainable way. Putting in the effort, building skills, and persevering over time is what creates lasting wealth and self-respect. It's not glamorous, but it's fulfilling.
5. **Making Money Work for You** – Once you've earned or saved enough, the smart path is to invest. Whether it's in businesses, stocks, or real estate, letting your money grow passively is how true financial freedom is achieved.

• • •

"Those who don't understand the failure, who never understand the
success"
| Gunjan Bhonde

• • •

The One Rule That Drives All Success

In this world, there exists a single, simple rule that lies at the heart of success a question that holds immense power. The more a person invests in understanding and leveraging this question, the more unstoppable and influential they become.

And that question, my friend, is:

• • •

"What's in it for me?"

• • •

At first glance, this may seem like a selfish or shallow question, but look deeper, and you'll realize its profound potential. Every individual, every action, and every decision are driven by the desire to answer this question whether they are aware of it or not.

Think about it:

- A customer buys a product because it solves a problem for them. *What's in it for me?* Value.
- A leader inspires their team by showing them the benefits of working toward a shared vision. *What's in it for me?* Growth and purpose.
- A person invests time and effort in a relationship. *What's in it for me?* Love, support, and connection.

This question is not about greed; it's about understanding motivations. It's about recognizing that every interaction be it business, personal, or social hinges on the ability to provide value to others.

The Secret to Mastering This Rule

True success comes not from asking this question only for yourself but from flipping the perspective:

"What's in it for them?"

When you focus on delivering value to others, you unlock doors to success that cannot be opened any other way. The key lies in aligning your goals with the needs and desires of those around you. By investing in their success, you naturally elevate your own.

- Entrepreneurs who understand their customers' needs build thriving businesses.
- Leaders who empower their teams create unstoppable organizations.
- Individuals who contribute to the lives of others build meaningful relationships and legacies.

Why This Question Matters

This rule transcends all areas of life career, relationships, business, and personal growth. It's not about manipulation or taking advantage. Instead, it's a tool to align interests, foster collaboration, and build a foundation for lasting success.

The man who masters this question, both for himself and others, becomes truly powerful. Because in the end, success isn't just about what you achieve for yourself it's about the impact you create for those around you.

So, my friend, I leave you with this thought:

Invest in this question. Study it. Apply it. Ask it not just for yourself, but for those you serve. And watch as it transforms your life.

Now, can you guess?

What's in it for you?

The first step to success is failure because failure is not a roadblock; it is a stepping stone that propels us forward. It teaches us resilience, patience, and the importance of perseverance. Failure is a powerful teacher, forcing us to confront our limitations, rethink our strategies, and refine our goals. Each time we fail, we learn something new about ourselves, our approach, and the challenges ahead. These lessons often become the building blocks for future success, shaping us into stronger, more capable individuals.

History is filled with examples of great minds who turned failure into triumph. Thomas Edison famously remarked that he didn't fail but instead found 10,000 ways that didn't work before inventing the light bulb. Similarly, J.K. Rowling faced countless rejections before her *Harry Potter* series became a global phenomenon. These stories remind us that failure is not the end; it is a necessary part of the process that allows us to grow, adapt, and eventually succeed.

Success isn't about avoiding failure it's about how we respond to it. Do we let it defeat us, or do we use it as fuel to try again with greater determination? When we shift our mindset to view failure as an opportunity for learning and self-improvement, it loses its power to hold us back. Instead, it becomes a catalyst for innovation and achievement.

The easiest way to make money lies in understanding human tendencies:

● ● ●

Men's lust.
Women's desire for beauty.
Elderly people's concern for health.
Children's need for education.
Rich people's fear of loss.
Poor people's desire to get rich quickly.

● ● ●

The first step to success is often the most crucial and transformative one: *deciding to begin.* Success doesn't come in a single moment; it's built over time, through consistent effort, learning from mistakes, and embracing personal growth. However, none of these things are possible without first making the choice to take action. It's easy to get caught up in dreams and aspirations, imagining what success might look like, but without the courage to take that initial step, all of those dreams remain just that dreams. Many people feel paralyzed by fear, doubt, or the enormity of what lies ahead, thinking they need to have everything figured out before they begin. But success isn't about having all the answers from the start it's about starting somewhere, no matter how small, and building from there.

The act of beginning, however simple it may seem, carries immense power. It's the point where you break through indecision and move forward, despite uncertainty. Whether it's writing the first line of a book, setting a small goal, or even making a commitment to yourself to try something new, that first action creates momentum. Once you take that step, the path ahead becomes clearer, and you're already on your way. It's also where you lay the foundation for discipline and persistence, both of which are essential for long-term success.

The first step also requires a shift in mindset a willingness to embrace the possibility of failure and to learn from setbacks rather than be discouraged by them. Success doesn't happen without obstacles, but it's how you respond to those challenges that defines your journey. When you decide to begin, you're not just committing to an action; you're committing to the process of growth, improvement, and learning. You acknowledge that success is not about perfection, but about progress. It's the courage to fail, to stumble, and to rise again that makes success truly achievable.

In a world filled with distractions and competing priorities, taking that first step is often the hardest part of the journey. The initial step is about confronting your fears, stepping out of your comfort zone, and putting your goals into motion. Once you've made the decision to begin, it's easier to keep going. Each small step you take builds confidence, reinforces your commitment, and propels you forward, even when the end goal seems far away. The key is to focus on the journey, rather than obsessing over the end result. Success is not a destination, but a process and the first step is where the process begins.

GyanVatsal Swami Ji beautifully explains the difference between *growth*, *progress*, and *success*. He states that increasing the turnover of a company, for example, from 50 crores to 100 crores or even 500 crores, is termed as **growth**. Growth is essentially the expansion of materialistic possessions and achievements.

However, when this growth is guided by **ethics**, such as discipline, honesty, and adherence to moral principles, it transforms into **progress**. Ethics serve as the foundation that ensures growth is not just quantitative but also qualitative.

Taking it a step further, Swami Ji explains that when this progress is coupled with **humanity**, **morality**, and **spirituality**, it becomes **success**. True success is not just measured by material achievements but by the values that shape them and the impact they leave on the world.

So, embrace failure as an essential part of your journey. Let it guide you, teach you, and inspire you to keep moving forward. Remember, every great success story begins with someone who was willing to fail, learn, and try again. Success isn't a destination; it's a journey one that's often paved with lessons learned through failure.

Imagine this: You're trying to make wine, but all you do is keep biting into the same sour grapes again and again, hoping the taste will magically transform. No matter how many times you try, the result is the same a mouthful of bitterness.

This is what happens when we repeatedly approach life's challenges the same way, expecting a different outcome. It's an illusion, a trap we all fall into at some point. **Doing the same thing over and over again and expecting different results is not just unproductive it's insanity.**

This is the **Law of Stagnation:** If you keep repeating the same failed actions, you will continue to get the same failed results.

The Trap of Repetition

Repetition feels comfortable. It's familiar, and it doesn't challenge us to step out of our comfort zones. But here's the harsh truth: **repeating what doesn't work will only reinforce failure.**

For example:

- If you're trying to lose weight but keep eating the same unhealthy food and skipping workouts, no amount of wishing will give you a fit body.
- If you're stuck in a toxic relationship and keep approaching it the same way, the cycle of frustration will never end.
- If you're failing at work but refuse to change your methods, your career will remain stagnant.

Repetition without progress is not determination it's **self-sabotage.**

Why We Keep Doing the Same Thing

So, why do we fall into this pattern?

1. **Fear of Change:** Trying something new is uncomfortable. We fear failure, so we cling to old habits, even when they clearly don't work.
2. **Lack of Awareness:** Sometimes, we don't even realize we're stuck in a cycle of repetition. We mistake activity for productivity.
3. **Hope Without Action:** We convince ourselves that if we just try harder or wait longer, things will eventually change. But hope without action is futile.

The Solution: Do Something Different

To break the cycle and achieve different results, you must be willing to change your approach. **You can't solve a problem with the same mindset that created it.**

The Law of Change

The Law of Change is simple: **If you want different results, you must take different actions.**

It applies to every area of life:

- **Health:** Try new diets or workout routines instead of sticking to what hasn't worked.

- **Relationships:** Communicate differently, set boundaries, or reevaluate toxic connections.
- **Career:** Learn new skills, network, or switch industries if necessary.

Key Takeaways

1. **Repetition without growth is a dead end.** Stop biting into the same sour grapes expecting wine.
2. **Identify what isn't working.** Be honest with yourself about your actions and their outcomes.
3. **Take bold steps.** Change is uncomfortable, but it's the only way to achieve something new.
4. **Learn from failure.** Every experiment, even the unsuccessful ones, brings you closer to success.

Remember: **Life rewards those who dare to change.**

Break the cycle. Step out of your comfort zone. The results you seek are waiting on the other side of your willingness to do something different.

• • •

"Learn the rules like a pro, so you can break them like an artist"
| Pablo Picasso, Spanish painter and sculptor

• • •

The truth is, money isn't simply earned it's a result of the value you bring to the world. At the lowest level, people make money through labor, selling their time and physical effort. In the middle class, money is earned through intellect, applying skills and knowledge to create value. At the highest level, wealth is generated through resources and power, leveraging influence and assets to multiply opportunities. Understanding this flow of value reveals why money follows certain people naturally those who strategically position themselves where value matters most. Building wealth requires mastering three key elements of relationships: paving the way by building connections, offering value at the right time, and maintaining strong relationships over time. Knowing what to say and when is equally critical: focus on work with superiors, talk about the future with subordinates, discuss opportunities with the less fortunate, and emphasize benefits with the wealthy. Wealth doesn't come from sheer labor but from skill and creativity, just as strength stems from wisdom rather than brute force. True success lies in understanding people, offering value, and navigating relationships with purpose, as these are the real drivers of financial and personal growth.

The true purpose of a business is not merely to make money, as many people believe, but to create and maintain long-lasting relationships with customers. A successful business focuses on meeting the needs of its customers, providing value, and fostering loyalty. The result of this approach is profit, but it comes as a byproduct of customer satisfaction and trust.

Many businesses fail due to low sales, and the primary reason for this is the lack of customer focus. Successful businesses, on the other hand, prioritize building a strong customer base, understanding their needs, and delivering consistently high-quality products or services. The key to business success lies in creating value for customers and establishing a brand that resonates with them, ensuring that they return time and again. By maintaining a customer-centric approach, businesses can thrive and grow, leading to long-term profitability and success.

In business, the key to success is taking calculated risks, not simply focusing on calculating profits. While profit is the ultimate goal, it cannot be achieved without making strategic decisions that involve some level of risk. A successful business owner understands that growth comes from stepping outside of comfort zones and making informed, thoughtful risks. These risks should be based on research, analysis, and experience, not on reckless decisions aimed solely at short-term gain.

By embracing calculated risks, businesses open themselves up to new opportunities, innovation, and long-term success. Focusing only on immediate profits may limit potential, whereas taking well-thought-out risks allows businesses to adapt, grow, and ultimately thrive in a competitive market. Risk, when managed wisely, becomes a powerful tool for achieving sustainable success.

Apple sells innovation, not phones. Rolex sells status, not watches. LEGO sells creativity, not toys. Nike sells motivation, not shoes. Coca-Cola sells happiness, not drinks. Tesla sells the future, not cars. These companies understand that success is not about merely selling products; it's about selling emotions, experiences, and aspirations. They have mastered the art of branding, creating connections with customers that go beyond the physical product.

In today's market, consumers are drawn to the values and emotions a brand represents, rather than just the functionality of its products. Successful brands tap into the deeper desires and motivations of their customers, offering them a sense of belonging, achievement, or joy. By selling an experience or a vision, rather than a mere product, these companies create lasting relationships with their customers, ensuring loyalty and long-term success.

The difference between a duck and a horse lies in their unique strengths and abilities. A duck can fly, swim, and walk under average conditions, but it cannot excel at any one of these tasks. On the other hand, a horse may not be as versatile, but it excels at one thing running. The horse's running ability is so extraordinary that it stands out as its greatest strength.

This comparison teaches us an important lesson: while being versatile is valuable, true excellence often comes from focusing on mastering one skill. The horse doesn't try to swim or fly; it dedicates itself to running, and as a result, it becomes the best in the world at it. Similarly, in life, putting all your energy into mastering one area where you can truly shine may lead to far greater success than spreading yourself too thin across many tasks.

If you can't run, if you can't walk, then by all means, you must keep moving forward. Life is full of challenges, and sometimes, the obstacles we face can make progress seem impossible. However, the key to overcoming these challenges is persistence. Even when you feel like you can't take a step forward in the way you had planned, the important thing is to keep moving, no matter how small the progress.

Whether you're crawling, walking, or moving at a slower pace, as long as you keep going, you're making progress. Success is not always about speed or perfection; it's about resilience and determination. No matter how difficult life becomes, always remember that forward movement, no matter how slow, is still progress toward achieving your goals.

There is a common pattern I have observed among rich and successful individuals, and it lies in three key skills: communication, closing, and copywriting.

1. Communication: The way they communicate, whether one-on-one or addressing a large audience, is truly remarkable. Their words carry confidence, clarity, and purpose, making their speech both engaging and impactful. They know how to connect with people, convey their ideas effectively, and leave a lasting impression.

2. Closing: Rich individuals are often exceptional persuaders and influencers. They have mastered the art of negotiation and know exactly how to get things done. Their ability to close deals, finalize decisions, and drive outcomes is unparalleled, making them stand out as effective leaders and achievers.

3. Copywriting: The choice of words they use while speaking, their writing style, and their presentation skills reflect a deep understanding of how to capture attention and inspire action. Their ability to craft messages with precision and intent ensures that their ideas resonate with others.

Your comfort zone isn't built around happiness it's built around safety. Your brain is incredibly skilled at shielding you from pain, failure, and rejection, but this protection often comes at the cost of your growth, ambition, and true fulfillment. Staying in this safe space might keep you unscathed, but it also keeps you from experiencing life fully. To truly grow, you must give yourself permission to try without clinging to expectations and to love without the need for possession. Like a ship in a harbor, you may feel secure in staying where it's safe, but that's not what ships are built for. You were meant to sail, to take risks, and to explore the vastness of life even if it means facing storms along the way. True happiness lies not in avoiding discomfort but in embracing the journey with courage and an open heart.

To become a perfect driver, you first have to get behind the wheel. The same principle applies to life you can't master something without starting. Success doesn't come from waiting for the perfect moment; it comes from taking the first step, learning as you go, and improving over time. Perfection is not a prerequisite; progress is what paves the road to success. So, don't let fear or doubt hold you back. Begin your journey, embrace the mistakes, and refine your skills along the way. Remember, the road to success isn't built by flawless beginnings but by consistent progress and persistence.

When you figure out who you truly are and what you want to do, and you devote your life to it with unwavering focus like a maniac who's all in something incredible happens. You begin to manifest the life you've envisioned. At this point, there's no room for half-hearted efforts or excuses. You become someone who doesn't just talk about dreams but actually turns them into reality. People around you will take notice because they'll see that you're serious, relentless, and unstoppable. The path may not always be easy, but when your determination is greater than your doubt, success becomes inevitable.

You wouldn't plant a seed and dig it up every few minutes to see if it has grown, so why do you keep questioning yourself and your hard work? Growth takes time, patience, and consistency. Doubting yourself or overthinking every step won't make the process any faster it will only delay your progress. Instead, trust in your decisions, keep nurturing your efforts, and have faith that the results will come. Remember, doubt has never led to greatness action does. So, stop second-guessing yourself and focus on moving forward. Keep watering your dreams, and let time do its magic.

Success is just like cooking a dish. When you step into the kitchen, the first thing you need is a recipe a proven guide to follow. You gather your ingredients, follow the instructions, and with time and practice, you master that dish. Once you've made it a few times, the process becomes second nature you no longer need to refer back to the recipe book. If someone compliments your cooking, you wouldn't call it magic or luck; you'd know it's the result of following a proven method. The same principle applies to success. There's no mystery to it just proven strategies and lessons passed down by those who've already walked the path. Successful people don't waste time reinventing the wheel; they learn from the experts, adapt proven methods, and refine them with their own efforts. Life is too short to figure everything out on your own, so seek wisdom from others, apply it, and carve your own path to success.

When someone becomes deeply obsessed with success, it often transforms into the answer for everything they once struggled with. Their doubts, insecurities, and failures begin to fade because their relentless pursuit creates momentum that drowns out self-doubt. Success becomes their armor, shielding them from criticism and their fuel, pushing them forward. But this obsession isn't about luck or shortcuts it's about focus, discipline, and unwavering belief. For such individuals, success is not just a goal but a way of rewriting their story, proving that determination can overcome any odds. When you align your actions with your ambitions, success becomes not just an outcome but the resolution to all that once held you back.

In business, choosing the right people to work with is crucial for success. Avoid getting involved with five types of individuals who can hinder your growth and progress. First, steer clear of the desperate ones those who are solely driven by immediate needs and lack long-term vision. They tend to make decisions out of fear, which often leads to poor outcomes. Secondly, chronic debaters can be exhausting. They constantly argue, challenge every idea, and waste time instead of finding solutions. Third, working with family and friends can be tricky, as personal relationships can cloud professional judgment and complicate business decisions. Fourth, people who don't respect you undermine your authority and influence. Respect is the foundation of any successful partnership. Lastly, latecomers are a sign of poor time management. Consistently arriving late or missing deadlines shows a lack of professionalism and can slow down progress. Surround yourself with individuals who are proactive, respectful, and aligned with your goals to create a business environment that thrives.

Every action you take in life is either propelling you toward your goals or moving you further away from them there is no such thing as a neutral action. If you're not actively making progress toward your aspirations, chances are, you're unintentionally drifting away from them. Whether it's your career, wealth, personal growth, or relationships, every choice and effort you make counts. The habits you form today will either bring you closer to the person you aspire to become or distance you from that vision. It's crucial to recognize that each small decision, no matter how insignificant it may seem, has an impact. Are you investing your time, energy, and resources in things that align with your dreams? Or are you letting distractions and inactivity take you off course? The key is intentionality. Every step, no matter how small, must be made with purpose to move you toward the life you want to create.

To live, a person doesn't just need food, water, or air; the most essential thing is *expectation*. While basic amenities are vital, it is the power of expectation that truly drives human existence. Expectation acts as a guiding light, giving us hope for a better future even in the most challenging times. The strength of expectation helps individuals face life's problems and uncertainties with resilience. It's this inner belief that tomorrow can be better, that things can improve, and that there's always the possibility of growth. No matter the hardships you face, never lose sight of your expectations. Just like a single ray of light can pierce the deepest darkness, a single spark of hope can transform your world. Keep your expectations high, for they hold the power to turn adversity into opportunity.

Aim for the moon, because even if you miss, you'll land among the stars. The higher you aim, the further you'll push yourself, stretching your limits and unlocking your true potential. Setting big goals is not just about achieving something extraordinary; it's about transforming who you are in the process. Most people hesitate to aim high out of fear of failure, fear of falling short, fear of what others might say. But this fear is what keeps them stuck in mediocrity, living a life far below their potential. When you aim low, like earning $5,000 a month, you can afford to indulge in lazy habits, procrastinate, or settle for minimal effort. There's no pressure to grow, no need to break past your comfort zone.

However, when you set a bold, seemingly impossible goal like earning $1 million a month it forces you to elevate your thinking and actions to a whole new level. You can no longer afford to waste time or energy. You'll wake up earlier, work harder, learn faster, and demand more from yourself. High goals force you to develop discipline, focus, and resilience, habits that will not only help you achieve your goal but will shape your character and carry over into every area of your life.

The beauty of aiming big is that even if you don't fully achieve the goal, you'll still end up far ahead of where you would have been had you settled for less. By striving for greatness, you'll find yourself in a much better position more skilled, more driven, and more accomplished than you ever imagined. The journey itself transforms you, and the progress you make becomes a reward in itself.

Donald Trump once said, ***"If you're going to be thinking, you may as well think big."*** This quote perfectly encapsulates the essence of ambitious goal-setting. If you're going to dream, dream without limits. If you're going to work, work towards something extraordinary. Life is too short to settle for mediocrity. Whether you hit the moon or land among the stars, aiming big ensures that you'll achieve far more than you would by playing it safe. So, dare to dream, dare to act, and let your ambition guide you to heights you never thought possible.

If you want to be truly successful, there are certain things you should avoid. First, you must understand that sleep and rest are luxuries that may not always be available during the pursuit of success. While rest is necessary for health, too much of it can derail your ambition. In the pursuit of greatness, there will be moments when you must push through exhaustion, because success doesn't wait for you to feel rested or refreshed. It's easy to become distracted by discomforts like hunger or illness, but these things shouldn't stop you from moving forward. If you wait for everything to be perfect if you rely on comfort and convenience, you'll find yourself stagnant, trapped in a cycle of laziness and inaction. The path to success is often filled with challenges, struggles, and pain. You might face fever, cold, or physical exhaustion, but if you stop, success will never come. There's no room for envy either; feeling jealous of others who are successful only hinders your progress. Instead, focus on your goals and push through

the discomfort. Success is earned through relentless effort and determination, and it won't come to those who are too comfortable or too fearful to take risks. True success requires constant drive, even when you feel weary or discouraged, because only through hard work and perseverance can you achieve the life you truly desire.

The difference between winners and losers is simple: winners take the first step. They don't make excuses or wait for the perfect moment. They just start, no matter how small the step may seem. Taking that first step is the key it doesn't mean you have to leap off a mountain, but rather take a small, deliberate action. When you take that first step, the next one becomes clearer, and the third step follows. It's like walking down a path where lights illuminate your way as you move forward, revealing the next step with each move you make. As you keep walking, surprises will unfold, and before you know it whether it's a week, a month, or a year later you'll look back and realize you've accomplished extraordinary things. People may call it luck, but it's not. Success comes from the consistent effort and the courage to begin. Top achievers in any field know this truth: the first step is the hardest, but once you take it, the rest will follow, and eventually, you'll find yourself among the top 10% in your field.

Dream so big that even your family thinks you're crazy. The bigger your dreams, the more powerful they become, because they push you beyond your limits and fuel your drive to achieve the impossible. As Albert Einstein once said, ***"The person with big dreams is more powerful than one with all the facts."*** It's not about having all the answers or knowing every detail; it's about having the courage to pursue what others may see as unattainable. Big dreams have the power to transform you, to challenge the status quo, and to inspire others. When you dream big, you tap into a limitless potential that moves you toward greatness, even if others doubt you along the way.

The difference between success and failure often lies in mindset. Successful people focus on growth, abundance, and solutions, while those who struggle tend to dwell on lack, loss, and limitations. It's not about circumstances but about how one thinks and approaches challenges.

The law of substitution plays a key role here. If you want to change your life, you must first change your thoughts. Replace negative thoughts with positive ones. Instead of worrying about failure, focus on opportunities. Instead of fearing risks, embrace them as chances to grow. The subconscious mind adjusts to what you consistently feed it, aligning your actions, feelings, and circumstances with your dominant thoughts.

Success begins when you stop being problem-centered and start being goal-centered. Think of what you want, not what you fear. The universe has a way of responding to your mindset if you think abundance, you attract abundance. If you think scarcity, you'll only see limitations. To truly unlock your potential, harmonize your thoughts, words, and actions with your vision of success. Remember, your mind is the most powerful tool you have use it wisely, and it will shape your reality.

The biggest enemy of success, in my opinion, can be summarized into three key obstacles that most people encounter on their journey toward achievement. These obstacles often prevent individuals from reaching their full potential, and unless they are consciously addressed and overcome, they can lead to a life of mediocrity.

• • •

"If you don't sacrifice for what you want, what you want becomes the sacrifice"
| Julie Thorn

• • •

1. The Comfort Zone

The first and most common enemy of success is the *comfort zone*. This is a mental and physical state where people settle into routines, habits, and behaviors that feel safe, familiar, and easy. While it may provide a sense of security, the comfort zone often leads to stagnation. People become complacent, resisting change, even when that change has the potential to improve their lives or help them grow. They fear the unknown, and instead of embracing new opportunities, they cling to what feels safe. The irony is that growth and success only occur when you step outside this zone. Unfortunately, studies show that approximately 80% of the population avoids change, even when it is beneficial, because the effort and uncertainty associated with change feel too intimidating.

2. Learned Helplessness

The second enemy is *learned helplessness*, a psychological state where individuals believe they are incapable of achieving certain goals or overcoming challenges, even when they have the ability to do so. This mindset is often the result of past failures or external influences, such as negative feedback, criticism, or a lack of support. Over time, people internalize the belief that they are not good enough, smart enough, or strong enough to succeed. As a result, they stop trying. This mindset is a silent killer of dreams, as it convinces individuals to settle for less than they are capable of achieving. Overcoming learned helplessness requires shifting your mindset from "I can't" to "I can," embracing a belief in your ability to grow, learn, and succeed despite challenges.

3. The Path of Least Resistance

The third and perhaps most deceptive enemy is the *path of least resistance*. This refers to the tendency to seek shortcuts, quick fixes, and easy ways out. People who fall into this trap often avoid hard work, discipline, and perseverance in favor of immediate gratification. They may dream big but fail to put in the consistent effort required to turn those dreams into reality. Success, however, is rarely achieved without struggle. It requires patience, resilience, and the willingness to take on challenges head-on. The pursuit of meaningful goals involves effort, sacrifice, and sometimes failure. Taking the easy way out might provide temporary comfort, but it will never lead to long-term success or fulfillment.

How to Overcome These Enemies

To achieve success, it is crucial to address and overcome these barriers:

- **Break Free from the Comfort Zone**: Challenge yourself daily to step outside your routines. Take risks, embrace discomfort, and seek opportunities to learn and grow. Success lies in the unknown, and the sooner you embrace change, the closer you'll be to achieving your goals.

- **Reframe Learned Helplessness**: Cultivate a growth mindset by focusing on possibilities rather than limitations. Surround yourself with supportive people, set small, achievable goals, and celebrate every step forward. Remember, failure is not the end it's a stepping stone toward success.

- **Avoid the Path of Least Resistance**: Commit to the hard work and dedication needed to achieve your goals. Embrace the challenges, as they build strength and character. Understand that shortcuts may save time in the moment but often lead to long-term regret and unfulfilled potential.

Success is not just about talent, resources, or luck. It's about consistently challenging yourself, believing in your abilities, and staying committed to the journey, no matter how tough it gets. By conquering these three enemies, you pave the way for growth, fulfillment, and extraordinary accomplishments.

You are your own worst enemy. Often, without even realizing it, you sabotage your own progress by wasting precious time dreaming about a distant future while neglecting the urgency and opportunities of the present moment. The truth is, the future is shaped by what you do today, yet many people fall into the trap of procrastination and daydreaming, convincing themselves that they are "planning" for the future when, in reality, they are avoiding action.

The present is where life happens it's the only moment within your control. However, instead of engaging fully in the now, you let distractions, doubts, and unnecessary worries take over. You involve yourself in tasks that provide little to no value, consuming your time and energy on what merely *fills* your day rather than what truly *moves* you forward. These behaviors not only hold you back but create a cycle of frustration, as you wonder why your dreams remain unfulfilled.

Every second wasted is a second of potential lost. Prioritize what truly matters. Commit yourself to the now, because the present is not just a fleeting moment it's the foundation upon which the future is built. You don't need to dream endlessly; you need to *do*.

In many fields, success and wealth are not necessarily tied to being the most skilled practitioner but rather to the ability to organize and utilize the skills of others effectively. For instance, a restaurant owner may not be the chef, yet they earn more than the chef by managing the business and creating opportunities for skilled chefs to showcase their talents. Similarly, a school owner may not be a teacher or possess the ability to teach, but they earn more than teachers by providing the infrastructure and resources for education. A hospital owner may not be a doctor, but they generate more income than doctors by running the institution and enabling healthcare professionals to deliver their expertise. Even in governance, many country presidents are not academic toppers or scholars, yet they lead entire nations through their leadership and decision-making abilities. One of the most vital skills in the modern world is the ability to identify, organize, and utilize talented individuals to achieve larger goals. Leadership, vision, and management often differentiate individuals who rise above others in terms of wealth and influence. It is not just about being skilled yourself but about creating an environment where others' skills contribute to collective success.

Unsuccessful people are often those who possess one unique yet crippling quality they harbor countless dreams but lack the will or discipline to work for them. They live in a fantasy world, endlessly imagining how their lives would change if they became someone great, achieved something extraordinary, or transformed the world. But here's the harsh truth: dreams without action are just illusions. Thinking about what you want to become or achieve means nothing if you're not willing to put in the relentless effort required to make it a reality.

These individuals tend to romanticize success, believing it will come easily or that mere desire is enough to manifest their goals. They think, *"If I achieve this or that, my life will change."* Yet, they fail to recognize the sweat, sacrifice, and struggle that lie behind every success story. The world doesn't reward wishful thinking it rewards those who work like slaves to their purpose.

If you truly want something, you must be prepared to give it your all. Success demands persistence, discipline, and an unshakable commitment to the grind. It means showing up even when you don't feel like it, sacrificing comfort, and pushing yourself beyond limits you didn't know existed. It's not enough to dream big; you must also act big.

Remember, the gap between where you are and where you want to be isn't bridged by thoughts it's bridged by action. Dreams only have value when paired with hard work. So, stop imagining and start doing. The world doesn't owe you success; you owe it to yourself to work for it.

Whenever a human faces hard times, their instinct is to search for work something that provides purpose, stability, and a way out of their struggles. In those moments of desperation, work becomes a beacon of hope, a solution to their problems, and a way to rebuild their life. However, the irony of life is this: once they find the work, they soon encounter the difficulties that come with it.

What initially seems like an answer to their prayers begins to test their patience, endurance, and willpower. The challenges, deadlines, responsibilities, and pressures of the job can often feel overwhelming. Many begin to question their ability to handle the difficulties and might even wonder if the struggle they faced without work was easier than the burden of the work itself. This cycle reflects a fundamental truth about life it's not free from challenges, no matter what path you choose.

The key, however, lies in perspective. Difficulties are not roadblocks; they are stepping stones. They exist to strengthen your character, sharpen your skills, and prepare you for greater opportunities. Every difficulty you face at work is an opportunity to learn and grow. The very hardships you encounter are what transform you into a more resilient, capable, and resourceful person.

Remember, no work worth doing will ever be free of obstacles. Success doesn't come from avoiding difficulties; it comes from embracing them and finding solutions. Hard times lead you to work, and work leads you to challenges but overcoming those challenges is what leads

you to success. So, instead of resisting the difficulties, accept them as part of your journey.

In the end, it's the struggle that shapes your strength and defines your destiny.

In my mind, I always carry the mindset that I am the best. It doesn't matter if others don't think so or if they've already dismissed me. Their opinions don't define me because success starts in your own mind. You have to believe in yourself first, even when no one else does.

You don't have to be the best in the world, but you should always strive to be the best version of yourself. Failure is inevitable, and what separates those who succeed from those who don't is how they respond to it. Many people fail before they even try because they're too consumed by the fear of judgment or criticism. But that fear? It's nothing more than a mental barrier. If you can conquer your mind, you can conquer anything.

Your mindset is everything. It determines how you approach challenges, how you handle setbacks, and how far you're willing to go. Instead of focusing on what others think or say, focus on your own growth and progress. When you believe in yourself, you carry a sense of confidence and determination that nothing can shake.

Remember, success is as much mental as it is physical. What you think about yourself and your abilities will shape your actions and, ultimately, your reality. So, keep telling yourself that you're the best not because you're competing with anyone else, but because you're constantly improving, learning, and growing.

In the end, it's not about being the best in the eyes of others. It's about knowing in your heart and mind that you've given your best effort and refused to let doubt or negativity hold you back. Believe it, embody it, and success will follow.

Keep doing it, even if you don't like it. Keep doing it, even if it makes you cry. Keep pushing forward, no matter how hard it feels. Success isn't born from comfort it's forged through perseverance, through the moments when everything inside you screams to stop, yet you choose to continue.

When you feel like giving up, remind yourself that the pain you're enduring now is temporary, but the rewards of your persistence will last a lifetime. Growth happens in discomfort. Strength is built in struggle. And resilience is born in those moments when you keep going, even when every step feels like a battle.

Crying doesn't mean you're weak it means you're human. Let the tears flow if they must, but don't let them stop you. Use them as fuel. Let every drop remind you of how badly you want to reach your goal. The greatest achievements in life come to those who keep going, who refuse to quit, and who show up for themselves every single day, no matter how they feel.

So, whether you're tired, frustrated, or full of doubt, keep doing it. Keep moving forward. Keep fighting for what you want. The struggle may be tough, but the results will make every tear, every hardship, and every sacrifice worth it. Remember, the only way to truly fail is to stop trying. Keep doing it you're stronger than you think.

The reality is, in the grand scheme of things, you might not feel very valuable. Society often measures worth by how much money you make or the title you hold, and it's easy to get caught up in comparing yourself to others. There are people out there the so-called "elite" who seem to get more, achieve more, and live more extravagantly, while you might feel like you're just getting by. But here's the truth: **your value isn't determined by external measures alone.**

If you want to elevate your life, you need to learn to work harder, not just at your job but also on yourself. Working hard at your job can help you make a living, but working hard on yourself can help you build a fortune. The difference lies in mindset and growth. Jobs give you stability, but personal development, skill-building, and strategic thinking create opportunities for extraordinary success. You don't just need to work harder you need to work smarter, invest in yourself, and focus on creating value that others can't ignore.

Remember, it's not about working tirelessly without direction. It's about working with purpose, building skills, and understanding that your ultimate fortune is a reflection of the effort you put into **who you are** and **what you can offer**. When you shift your focus from just making a living to creating value, the game changes. Life rewards those who think beyond the basics, who take risks, and who are willing to invest time and energy into their own growth.

You might feel undervalued now, but you're not destined to stay that way. Use this reality as fuel to push yourself forward. Learn new things, hone your craft, and commit to personal excellence. Your value will grow when you start recognizing your potential and taking deliberate steps to unlock it. You're not just working for a paycheck you're building a future, a legacy, and a version of yourself that no one can ignore. Keep striving, and remember: **you are your greatest investment.**

To become the best in your field, it all starts with **one day of focused effort.** Imagine dedicating an entire day morning to evening, for 24 hours to learning everything you can about your chosen field. If you truly commit to that, immersing yourself in knowledge, skills, and insights, you'll already know more than most people around you. This is how the journey begins.

From that one day, you gain an edge a foundation that sets you apart. When you continue to build on that knowledge consistently, you'll start to stand out even more. People will notice your growth and expertise. Over time, you'll surpass those closest to you. You'll move from being knowledgeable within your immediate circle to becoming one of the top 40 in your community, then the top 400 in your city, and eventually the top 4,000 in your region.

But don't stop there. With relentless focus and a commitment to self-improvement, you'll rise to the top 400,000 in your country, and from there, the possibilities are endless. This is how individuals become national and even global leaders in their field. It all begins with that **one day of intentional effort.**

Remember, greatness is not achieved overnight, but it does begin with a single, deliberate step. Every expert you admire today started as a beginner who chose to focus, learn, and grow. Start with **one day** use it wisely. Dedicate it to mastering something important in your field, and let that momentum carry you forward.

Your journey to becoming the best might seem overwhelming, but breaking it down into focused, purposeful days makes it achievable. One day becomes a week. One week becomes a month. And before you know it, you've surpassed even your own expectations. It's not about waiting for the perfect moment it's about starting now, taking consistent steps, and building a future that puts you among the best in the world. **Start today, and make it your best day.**

Success is not a gift that the world hands to you; it is something you create for yourself. It is self-made, built brick by brick through the daily battles you fight within yourself. Every single day, you are faced with two choices: to move forward into the **growth zone** or to retreat into the comfort of the **familiar.** Success is not achieved by staying comfortable; it is forged in the fire of hard decisions, consistent effort, and unwavering commitment to self-improvement.

The path to success is far from easy it is demanding, it requires sacrifice, and it often brings pain. You will have to give up certain comforts, endure sleepless nights, and face moments of doubt when it feels like no one notices your efforts. But that is exactly what makes success so powerful and fulfilling. When you look back at the empire you've built, you'll realize that it was the **struggle** that shaped you. Every sacrifice you made, every hardship you endured, contributed to your strength and character.

Struggle is not your enemy it is your greatest teacher. Without struggle, there is no growth, and without growth, there is no success. Embrace the challenges, because they are what transform you into the person capable of achieving your dreams. Remember, the pain and sacrifices you endure today are temporary, but the rewards they bring are exponential. **For every ounce of struggle, life will give you tenfold in return.**

So, don't fear the hard times. Don't shy away from the uphill battles. Lean into them with determination and grit, knowing that they are essential steps on your journey to greatness. Success isn't handed out freely; it's earned through resilience, discipline, and the courage to keep going, even when the odds are against you. **Let every struggle remind you that you are becoming stronger, smarter, and more capable and that the best is yet to come.**

Imagine you board the wrong train, thinking it will take you to your destination. At first, you don't realize it's the wrong train, but when you do, you're faced with a decision. You can either step off at the next station and take corrective action paying for a return ticket, wasting precious time, and making up for your mistake or you can stay on the train and continue moving in the wrong direction, farther from where you truly want to be. Either way, the cost of a wrong decision becomes evident your time, money, and energy are wasted, none of which can be fully recovered.

Now, think of this scenario as a metaphor for life. Choosing the wrong train is like succumbing to distractions and comfort zones endless hours on social media, fleeting temporary relationships, or indulging in unproductive habits. These things often seem harmless or even enjoyable in the moment, but they steer you away from your true goals and purpose. Just like the wrong train, they lead you further from your desired destination.

What's worse is when you know you're on the wrong train but fail to act. You ignore the warnings, convincing yourself that staying put is easier than going through the effort of returning to the right path. This is where the real danger lies every moment you continue moving in the wrong direction, you dig yourself deeper into the wrong destination. The journey back becomes harder, costlier, and more time-consuming.

The truth is, the longer you delay correcting your course, the more you lose not just time and money but also opportunities that may never come again. Life, unlike a train journey, doesn't offer infinite chances to start over. The clock keeps ticking, and every moment you waste in the wrong direction is a moment you could have spent building the future you truly desire.

So, what should you do? The answer is simple but not easy: *Step off the train. Correct your course. Accept the cost of your mistakes and focus on moving forward in the right direction.* It may be uncomfortable, it may require sacrifice, but it is far better than staying stuck in a situation that takes you further from your dreams.

Learn to identify the "wrong trains" in your life whether it's toxic relationships, unproductive habits, or distractions and have the courage to step away from them. Yes, you'll need to pay a price for your mistakes, but the price of staying on the wrong path is far greater. Choose wisely, because the destination you reach is a direct result of the path you take. And remember, no matter how far you've traveled in the wrong direction, it's never too late to turn around and start heading toward the right one.

• • •

Success doesn't care about excuses.

• • •

Growth doesn't happen in a straight line.

If you want to change your life, excuses mean nothing. The only thing that matters is staying consistent and disciplined, no matter what.

The Mindset Shift

Understand this: success is less about talent and more about persistence. It's not about who works the hardest for a day it's about who keeps going for months and years.

Think of a dripping faucet: one drop of water seems insignificant, but over time, those drops can fill an entire bucket. Your daily efforts work the same way. Small, consistent actions lead to extraordinary results.

Your Life Is in Your Hands

If you want to change your life, it starts with one decision:

Commit to the process, stay consistent, and refuse to quit.

You don't need to be extraordinary to succeed you just need to show up every day and give your best effort. No excuses. No shortcuts. Just consistent discipline.

Success isn't for the lucky; it's for the determined.

So, start today. Start small. But whatever you do, don't stop.

• • •

"Wisdom has been chasing you, but you have always been faster"
| Uncle Iroh, Fictional character

• • •

The Journey of Failure, Hard Work, and Success: Lessons from the Chinese Bamboo

Success is often compared to the growth of a Chinese bamboo tree a process that teaches us patience, perseverance, and the importance of building strong foundations. When you plant the seed of a Chinese bamboo tree, nothing remarkable happens at first. For four years, you must water the seed, provide it sunlight, and nurture it with care. Yet, during those years, there is no visible sign of growth above the ground. It's easy to get discouraged, to feel as though your efforts are wasted.

But in the fifth year, something extraordinary happens. Within just six weeks, the bamboo tree shoots up to an astonishing height sometimes over 80 feet tall. This rapid growth is not a miracle; it is the result of years of unseen hard work beneath the surface. During those initial years, the bamboo was growing its roots spreading deep and wide into the ground to create a strong foundation that could support its towering height. Without those roots, the bamboo would never stand tall.

Just like the bamboo, our progress is often invisible in the beginning. You may put in countless hours of hard work, face failure after failure, and feel as though nothing is changing. But what's really happening is that you are laying the groundwork for your future success. Each failure strengthens your roots. Each struggle teaches you resilience. Each setback pushes you to grow outside of your comfort zone.

The first step of success is about taking action in the face of uncertainty, trusting that each step you take brings you closer to your goals. Whether that first step is big or small, it is the start of something powerful, and it is often the most important decision you'll make on your path to success. When you decide to begin, you take ownership of your dreams and start transforming them into reality, one step at a time.

CHAPTER XV

Changing the World

• • •

"To change the world, change yourself first "
| Gunjan Bhonde

• • •

Changing the world is not an overnight endeavor it requires time, patience, and an unwavering commitment to growth and improvement. As the saying goes, *"Rome wasn't built in a day,"* and similarly, creating meaningful change demands persistence and consistent effort over time. The journey to change the world begins with a single step, and that step starts within you. Before you can inspire others or influence the world around you, it's essential to transform yourself first. Self-reflection, self-discipline, and a desire to improve are the seeds of true change.

When you cultivate good habits, embrace learning, and develop a mindset rooted in compassion and integrity, you naturally become a force for good. Your actions and choices, no matter how small they may seem, have the power to inspire others. Doing good work for society doesn't always mean grand gestures; sometimes, it's about the little things helping a neighbor, spreading kindness, or contributing your time and skills to make your community better. Each of these acts creates a ripple effect, touching lives and inspiring others to do the same.

Changing the world is a concept that often feels overwhelming or distant, as if it requires grand gestures or a singular moment of brilliance. However, the truth is that transformation often begins with small, deliberate actions that ripple outwards, creating an impact that can grow and spread over time. The notion of changing the world is rooted in the idea that individual actions matter, and that even the smallest steps can make a significant difference when combined with the efforts of others. It's about fostering a mindset of progress, where each positive change no matter how minor contributes to a larger, collective effort to improve the world we live in.

At its core, changing the world begins with a shift in perspective. It involves understanding that the world is shaped by the choices we make, both individually and collectively. Change can happen when we challenge old ways of thinking, break down barriers of injustice, or encourage a more inclusive and compassionate society. It starts with recognizing the inequalities or problems that exist, whether they are related to poverty, education, the environment, or human rights, and actively seeking solutions to address them. In this way, changing the world is not a single event, but an ongoing process one that requires persistence, resilience, and a long-term vision.

One of the most powerful ways to change the world is through the power of compassion and empathy. Acts of kindness, no matter how simple, can have profound effects. When we show understanding and support to others, especially those who are marginalized or struggling, we create a ripple effect that promotes love and solidarity. A single act of kindness can inspire others to do the same, building a network of goodwill that spreads throughout communities, cities, and even nations. This is how global movements of change are often born through the collective efforts of individuals who are united by a common vision and who understand the power of empathy to break down walls and build bridges.

In the age of information and technology, changing the world has also become a shared responsibility. Social media, digital platforms, and online communities allow us to communicate and organize in ways that were once unimaginable. From climate activism to social justice campaigns, people across the globe are now able to unite for causes that matter to them, amplifying their voices and pushing for systemic change. In this interconnected world, we are more aware of the challenges faced by others, and this awareness can be a catalyst for global movements that demand change on a larger scale.

Education and innovation also play crucial roles in shaping a better future. Knowledge empowers individuals to make informed decisions, solve problems, and create new possibilities. When people are equipped with the tools to think critically, create solutions, and envision a better world, they are more likely to contribute positively to their communities and to society at large. Innovations in technology, medicine, and sustainable practices have the potential to revolutionize industries, improve lives, and address the most pressing challenges of our time, such as climate change, health care, and global poverty.

However, the journey to changing the world requires not just action, but reflection. It is important to understand that while we strive to change external conditions, we must also be willing to examine and change our own behaviors, attitudes, and habits. True change begins from within by questioning biases, expanding our worldview, and adopting values that prioritize fairness, sustainability, and the well-being of all. In doing so, we are not just contributing to a better world, but also evolving into individuals who can inspire others through our actions and choices.

Remember, last change takes time, but with dedication and perseverance, even the smallest efforts can lead to extraordinary outcomes. So, start within yourself, led by example, and let your actions pave the way for a better, more harmonious world. Change yourself, and you'll find that the world begins to change with you.

Some men realize their purpose at 18, some at 30, and some may go their entire lives without ever realizing it. The truth is, as a man, no one else can truly solve your problems or fulfill your dreams for you. Your challenges, your aspirations, and your responsibilities belong solely to you. No one is going to hand you a free ticket to success, and there are no shortcuts in life. Whatever you desire, whatever you envision for yourself, will require relentless effort and dedication.

You must understand that being alone in this journey doesn't mean you're powerless it means you're the hero of your own life. No one is coming to save you, and that's okay because you have the ability to save yourself. You hold the pen to write your own story, create your own rules, and carve out the path you want to walk. The battles you face, the struggles you endure, and the victories you achieve are yours to claim. Being the hero of your life means taking ownership of everything your decisions, your failures, your progress, and your success. It's about realizing that the power to transform your life lies within you. The road will not be easy, but every challenge you overcome will shape you into a stronger, wiser, and more capable version of yourself.

Remember, no one else can define you, and no one else can live your story. So, rise up, fight for your dreams, and create the life you've always imagined. The journey may be difficult, but the reward of knowing you built it all on your own will be worth everything. You are not just a man you are the author, the warrior, and the victor of your own life.

Dex Torricke-Barton, in his TEDx talk *How to Change the World – A Practical Guide*, provides insights on leadership and how to create meaningful change in the world. He emphasizes that to make real progress, we must begin by examining our own perspectives and defining the world we aim to change. By using different world maps as metaphors, he highlights how the way we see the world can be distorted, and it's crucial to recognize the reality of global issues like hunger and lack of access to basic needs before embarking on solutions.

He advocates starting small, like trading a paperclip for a house, which illustrates that large goals require incremental steps and practical actions. Torricke-Barton also stresses the importance of defining what truly matters to you rather than simply following popular trends. In this regard, he references Henry Ford's philosophy of building what he believed in, even if it wasn't what customers initially wanted.

The speaker also touches on the value of collaboration, pointing out that collective action often leads to more profound impact than solitary efforts. Communications play a key role in this process products or ideas must be communicated effectively to make a difference. He highlights the importance of understanding human emotions and the ethical context behind data, stressing that data alone doesn't solve problems, but rather the human understanding of it does.

Lastly, Torricke-Barton underscores the need for leaders to recognize when to step back, knowing when to surrender and when to shift focus to where one can create more value. His talk encourages a mindset of unity rather than division, aiming for collective progress rather than creating conflict.

This practical guide emphasizes that real change comes from understanding the world as it is, breaking down goals into actionable steps, and collaborating with others in a way that transcends individual egos or divisive tactics.

Admiral William H. McRaven delivered an inspiring commencement speech to the University of Texas class of 2014, sharing ten valuable lessons from his Navy SEAL training that can help anyone change the world. He began by emphasizing the importance of starting each day by making your bed. This simple task provides a sense of accomplishment, builds discipline, and reinforces the idea that little things matter. Even on tough days, returning to a neatly made bed serves as a reminder that tomorrow can be better.

McRaven highlighted the power of teamwork, stating that no one can succeed alone. Drawing from his training, he shared how synchronized effort and collective determination were vital for his team to navigate the challenges of paddling through high surf. He also stressed that success is not determined by physical stature or background, but by perseverance and heart. The best-performing crew in his class, known as the "Munchkin Crew," was made up of individuals who were small in size but large in determination.

Adversity, McRaven noted, is inevitable. He described the "sugar cookie" drill, where students had to endure being cold, wet, and sandy all day, no matter how perfect their efforts had been. This lesson taught resilience and the importance of moving forward even when life feels unfair. Similarly, the dreaded "circus," an extra two hours of physical training for those who failed to meet standards, built strength and resilience over time, reinforcing the idea that failure is a necessary step toward growth.

Innovation and boldness were also key lessons. McRaven recounted how a student broke a long-standing obstacle course record by taking a risk and sliding down the rope headfirst, demonstrating that sometimes unconventional approaches can lead to extraordinary results. He also shared the importance of standing firm in the face of fear, using the metaphor of sharks circling during ocean swims to encourage courage and confidence in challenging situations.

McRaven reminded the audience that composure in the darkest moments is crucial. He described swimming under a ship's keel, where complete darkness and deafening noise test even the strongest individuals. In those moments, one must remain calm and rely on their training and inner strength. He also highlighted the power of hope, recounting a moment during "Hell Week" when his team, submerged in freezing mud, began singing together. That single act of hope lifted everyone's spirits and gave them the strength to endure.

Finally, McRaven emphasized the importance of never quitting. In SEAL training, there is a brass bell in the center of the compound. Ringing it signals a trainee's decision to quit and walk away. McRaven encouraged the graduates to resist the temptation to give up, no matter how difficult life becomes.

Changing the world is about creating a legacy of kindness, equality, and progress. It is about standing up for what is right, even when it is difficult, and working toward solutions that benefit everyone, especially those who are most vulnerable. Every small action, every conversation, and every effort to do better can contribute to a world that is more just, compassionate, and sustainable. It is a journey that requires patience, commitment, and the belief that together, we can create meaningful change. The world will change not only through the big movements but also through the millions of individual actions that make up the collective force of humanity striving for a brighter future.

Volume II: Facing Fear

Coming Soon...